The Mardi Gras Syndrome

To Marcie

wishing you
all joy & whatever

Joan Timmerman

THE MARDI GRAS SYNDROME

Rethinking Christian Sexuality

Joan H. Timmerman

CROSSROAD | NEW YORK

To all those men and women, ministers of all churches,
pastors, parents, and lovers who are doing Wednesday's work:
rediscovering for themselves and for each other the
fullness of Christian love.

1984
The Crossroad Publishing Company
370 Lexington Avenue, New York, N.Y. 10017

Library of Congress Cataloging in Publication Data
Timmerman, Joan H.
  The Mardi Gras syndrome.
  1. Sex—Religious aspects—Christianity. I. Title.
BT708.T55   1984   261.8'357   83-26286
ISBN   0-8245-0645-6

A medieval document admonishes Christian married couples to abstain from sexual intercourse on Thursday in honor of the Lord's Supper, Friday to commemorate the crucifixion, Saturday in honor of the Blessed Virgin Mary, Sunday for the Resurrection, and Monday for the Poor Souls. . . .

D.S. Bailey
The Man-Woman Relation in Christian Thought

What woman, having ten silver coins, if she loses one coin, does not light a lamp and sweep the house and seek diligently until she finds it? And when she has found it, she calls together her friends and neighbors, saying "Rejoice with me for I have found the coin which I had lost."

Luke 15:9

The reign of God is like a buried treasure which a man found in a field. He hid it again, and rejoicing at his find went and sold all he had and bought that field.

Matthew 13:44

Contents

Preface

My concern with what may be called the "Mardi Gras Syndrome" in Christian theory and practice regarding sexuality grew out of my special interest in Christian sacramentality. Sacramentality, the capacity of the world to reveal and the person to apprehend the mysterious presence of God, is central to theology. And it would seem that human sexuality ought to be viewed as participating in the revelatory power of nature and in the sacred character of matter. But the deeper I went into the study of theology, the clearer it became that sexuality had been excluded on various grounds from those things that were valued and cultivated as capable of leading one to God. The medieval document that admonished Christians to avoid conjugal relations—on Thursdays in honor of the Last Supper, on Fridays in commemoration of the crucifixion, on Saturdays in honor of the Blessed Virgin Mary, on Sundays because of the resurrection, and on Mondays for the sake of the poor souls in purgatory—is just one example of the tendency to regard the "giving up" rather than the loving use of sexuality as conducive to holiness. One can imagine a "Thank God it's Tuesday" celebration to rival any of our contemporary Friday night rituals of relaxation.

But a more serious effect attached itself to the mandates imposing extraordinary restraint on Christians. That effect can be called a syndrome because it represents a number of conflicting attitudes that occur together to produce a certain dis-ease or alienation regarding sexuality. It might be called a "Mardi Gras" syndrome because it is characterized by a feast or famine mentality. Not wholesome and responsible integration with the rest of life but artificial restraint coupled with periodic overindulgence characterizes this approach. Sexuality becomes an increasingly fearsome and fascinating aspect of being human. A syndrome overtakes what should have been as healthy and saving a reality as any other in incarnate life. This book has grown out of my attempts to explain the inconsistencies and resolve the contradictions in the traditional Christian approach to sex.

Much that is here is common knowledge, available in one form or another for some time. However, old habits still perdure, and the message that may seem commonplace to some is eagerly sought and gratefully received by others whose sexual lives have suffered from insufficient or inaccurate understandings of how sexuality is to be integrated into a full and liberating human life. Suggestions for additional reading have been included for the convenience of the reader. Some of these books and articles are well known; others less so. Many of them have influenced my thinking and rethinking on this subject.

My thoughts on these questions have been stimulated, ordered, changed, and developed by the many audiences who have engaged me to talk about theology and sexuality. I acknowledge them with gratitude, for they have tested and moderated and, in some cases, sharpened both my perceptions and the language in which I express them. I am aware that reflection on sexual questions, as on other matters that concern theologians, is done within a community and is tested by the experience of that community. I am grateful for having been invited, cajoled, sometimes almost forced into helping the community think through bothersome issues. These experiences have convinced me that, while the information and point of view contained in this book is not totally new, the need for its recovery in the lives of individual Christians has been newly perceived. It is my hope that, when rediscovered, a Christian value for sexual love and pleasure will be truly won. In order to avoid sexist language, I have varied the pronouns *he* and *she* so that both are used, neither exclusively. This is simply a practical way to avoid the repetitious and awkward he/she construction while still recognizing the experience and contribution of both men and women.

I wish to acknowledge the students who have participated in my twelve years of learning about human sexuality as a teacher of it. For the first five years, my course was taught under the rubric "Sexuality and the Sacred"; for the last seven, it has been in an interdisciplinary course on "Human Sexuality." To my co-teacher in the latter endeavor, Pat Bartscher, of the Nursing Department at the College of Saint Catherine, in St. Paul, Minnesota, I am indebted almost as much as to our thoughtful and challenging students.

Finally, I owe a word of recognition to those individuals who have been particularly important, not necessarily to this book, but to my education and my desire to be of service to Christian theology. Preeminent among them are Edward Ave-Lallemant; Bernard Cooke; William J. Kelly, S.J.; Justus George Lawler; John H. Nota, S.J.; Sean O'Riordan, C.SS.R.; and Margaret Shekleton, S.D.S.

Introduction

The study of human sexuality is as much a part of the human project as the study of language, reason, or religion. Unfortunately, until quite recently, it has been a much neglected field for study, though not for discussion and polemic. My interest in sexuality as a theological question came by way of my teaching the theology of the sacraments. From analysis of human symbolic action, from study of universality of religious experience and its description in sexual images, and from observation of the religious rituals surrounding puberty and marriage, a clear conclusion emerged: The religious value of human sexuality, while implicit in rites, practices, and morals, needs to be stated more directly and forthrightly. Human sexuality participates in the sacred; it is capable of revealing God and God's action in human life, and of transforming human existence from an isolated and disconnected experience to one of unity and ecstasy. It is, of course, open to the demonic as well, and is capable of destroying personalities and lives if its power is abused.

Nonetheless, human sexuality does *not* reveal itself as a profane activity, although it has come to be regarded as such in contemporary life. Some scholars have suggested that the modern person, for whom most vital experiences have been desacralized, is incapable of experiencing sexuality as it was experienced in archaic cultures. For primitive peoples, the principal physiological functions could become sacraments—for them the world was sacred, and every human experience was capable of being transfigured.

Is the experience of a sanctified sexual life no longer available in our contemporary society? This question seems to me to be extremely important. If it must be answered with a yes, then human beings today have the right to know what a truncated and deprived experience of sexuality has been available to them —and the right to look for more.

I see this book as a very small part of the search that is going on in both religious and secular spheres for a more meaningful, which is to say, a more sacred, sexual life. It will attempt to re-establish our sexual capacities and activities among those realities that sanctify human life and further human development. It will also attempt to indicate where insights were lost and truths forgotten, in the bibilical and Christian traditions, insofar as these losses influenced attitudes toward the body, sexuality, woman, and the earth. The richness of the present moment for this tradition is that it is a moment in which a valuable piece of human life, like the coin in the parable, can be recovered. The loss can be shown to be unfortunate but temporarary; the over-whelming spirit of the tradition can be shown to be one that affirms the good of nature, the body, ecstasy, and the dignity of the human person.

The days of the "Mardi Gras Syndrome" in Christian thinking about sex are numbered. The understanding of sexual pleasure and bodily expression that has been recovered in our time re-jects the association of such pleasure solely with chaos, indulgence, and disorder. The response of a Mardi Gras mentality to sex was to confine it to certain times, states of life, and explicit motivations. But sexuality is integral to human nature and necessary for full human development. The unintended effect of such "containment" measures has been immaturity and vio-lent, explosive episodes, not to mention the shriveling of indi-viduals' capacity for love. No longer need Christian sexual lives be relegated to the Tuesdays of the week or the Mardi Gras periods of the year, with secrecy and guilt-feelings poisoning the less confined forms. Christ came that they may have life and have it more abundantly.

While the question of sex is often considered a "women's issue,"[1] the perspective of this book is not that of feminism in any narrow sense, but rather of social justice. The larger context within which all important contemporary issues need to be seen is that of human development — in international, local, and individual concerns. And human development is a concept that includes but far transcends that of human rights, material well-being, or personal self-fulfillment. It recognizes human sexuality, its expression and control, to be of prime social and political significance. It insists that any sexual ethic which is limited to the biological or the individualistic is grossly inadequate and ultimately unjust.

I hope to suggest that more good human sex, and less exploitive sex, will advance the human race toward the participation in grace and redemption that Christians call salvation. When human sexuality is finally connected with love, then we will witness a sexual revolution worthy of the name. What has been called our sexual revolution may be widespread but it is often dehumanizing because casual sex can be used for the avoidance of intimacy rather than its cultivation. When it achieves its potential, human sexuality creates connections — connections with self, nature, and God, as well as with others. I hope to show that our concept of human sexuality has been impoverished and, consequently, our experiences are often those of failure, exploitation, fear, and guilt. Those who fear that our times are too affirming of sexual relations may be fearing the wrong thing. We have gone not to the opposite extreme from the recent past but to another version of the same extreme — to an attitude that views sex as profane rather than as sacred, as privately rather than socially significant, and as a threat to salvation rather than a cause of it.

The intent of this book is, therefore, to be *theological* in the broad sense of considering all things in their relationship to God, to be *radical* in the sense of challenging entrenched presuppositions, and to be *exploratory* in attempting to relate new information and data to a previously closed question.

Scholarship and reflection on human sexuality, while aiming at objectivity and universal validity, is invariably affected by the life story and life project of the writer. This is true of any theme that deals with human matters. I have tried scrupulously to raise my personal assumptions to the level of consciousness and then either to bracket them or to identify them for the reader.

I hope that my attempt to pose the question of sexuality under a new heading, that of social justice and interrelationship, will help to free the discussion of sexuality from the false polarizations of the past.

1·

Thursday: Losing the Coin
Sex, Sacred or Profane?

Sex is a *sacramental* reality. By sex I mean the whole range of feeling and acts that embodied persons engage in in their processes of relating to each other, from walking around museums together to hand holding, kissing, necking, petting, intercourse of various kinds, and afterplay. I do *not* mean solely that part of feeling that has been called venereal pleasure or lust or eros—this would connote less than the truth. I also do not mean solely the genital activity that characterizes procreative intent. That is also less than the truth.

A great breakthrough in our theological thinking about this topic occurs when it dawns on us that our sexuality is in our *being* and not just in the functions of certain of our organs. There is sexuality in each and every word and act, just as there is spirituality in each and every act of the incarnate persons we are. Once we realize this, it makes no sense to try to single out a section of ourselves as the focus of our sin and guilt; nor does it make sense to imagine sexuality as a separable section, a kind of luxury that we can deny we have and refuse to deal with in any conscious way. Our sexuality is our embodiment and it pervades every act of our body-selves. To be embarrassed about it or ashamed of it would be as absurd and self-defeating as shame at our noses or hands or relatedness.

The word *sacramental* refers to the function that all of nature has borne since the revelation of God in Christ and is derived from the Latin word for symbol. In this context, a sacramental reality, a symbol of God's love, is any action or thing that delivers to us the experience of God's presence or places us in touch with the basic mystery—the mystery that we are loved by God. Happily, there is today a stress on the religious dimension of ordinary human experiences. This stress does not deny God's freedom to intervene in special ways, but it cultivates an awareness of the reality, the mystery, that permeates all human events.

About all we can do at this point is appeal to our experience, including our sexual experience. Is there not a dimension of mystery that undergirds our experience? At the depths of the significant things that we do or undergo, is there not an occasional awareness of something that could be called the More, the Whole, the Transcendent, the Other? Any human interaction is and should be capable of revealing our relationship to this mystery. When I play with children I grasp *in* and *through* the playing a momentary glimpse of the "wonder of it all," the ultimate gift of love. When my father sits by the side of the lake, in and through the watching he is lost in an awareness of the rhythms of life and death and of his own living inside this reality. Our *faith* is faith that the ultimate loving reality, the mystery, is there all around us. Our *experience* is that in and through these common but special human interactions we are catapulted into an awareness of our relationship with that reality.

Theology has traditionally affirmed that certain experiences reveal the source and destiny of human life. The accompanying of Christ in his suffering, and the experience that he through his Spirit remained with them as consoler, strengthener, and advocate were such experiences to the disciples of Jesus—men and women—whose stories are recounted in the New Testament. When we look at the small pieces that made up those stories, we see that they are actions like ours—dining, talking, caressing with oil, caring for each other. These actions made up the rites and ceremonies that Christians soon began to do in the name of the Lord Jesus, and that they called sacraments. They were sacramental because in doing them the mystery of God's love revealed in Jesus was experienced once again as transparent, as the reality of the water, the food, the anointing, and the forgiving. The human things aren't *done away with* to get at the mystery—rather, it is *in* and *through* them that the love of God is made present and active in the life of this people.

But why is it that some types of experience have not brought with them an awareness of this holy mystery within which we "live and move and have our being." Sexual experience has by and large been characterized (at least by the writers who achieved ascendancy in the Christian theological tradition) as at worst a place of demonic impulses and forces that pull us against our will and as at best an ambiguous reality that inspires fear, guilt, humor, and some often regretted pleasure. For traditional religious humanity, prior to the widespread desacralization of sex, sex was an experience of the divine; but for modern Christian and post-Christian Westerners, it is often opaque and has little significance beyond the two individuals, their bodily pleasures, and their possible offspring.

Why should this be so? Where was a pearl of such great price lost? Why should an integral aspect of our humanity be excluded from our religious experience? After all, if faith is the attitude that tells us how much we're going to see, why do we see so little in sex? The question moves one to reflect on the historical sources to find out if the pearl might yet be recovered.

In the Gospels two images are used, one female, one male, that seem appropriate to the attempt to appreciate how sex is sacramental. There was a woman who swept the house from attic to alley to find a coin that she had lost. She found it, and called her neighbors to celebrate her good (rewon) fortune. There is another story about a man who heard about a field in which a treasure was buried. To those who had no knowledge of the treasure it seemed a foolish idea, but after selling all he had and buying the field, he found the treasure. He won not only the treasure, but praise from the skeptics.

The theological reconsideration of sex has gained much of its impetus from the renewal of biblical study and improved historical methods but it is also indebted to the feminist movement and the entrance into theological schools of large groups of men and women who do not interpret purity to mean sexual abstinence. They find enough clues in their houses and fields to make them devote their lives to the critical study of the tradition.

In Old Testament times, sex was a prominent symbol of union with the gods and goddesses in the cult religions which surrounded Israel. This led the Israelites to reactionary views on any attempt to relate sexual practices to worship or to the spiritual (religious) life. Yahweh, God of the Hebrews, was conceptualized as a creator without consort who, contrary to the creation stories of the other religions, brought forth all of life by word only, without any sexual partnership or imagery: in this creating there was no paradigm for human sexual life. Yahweh was sole sovereign, leader of the chosen people in their historical exodus and journey, but the symbols of his presence and his power were historical symbols not symbols from nature. War, not sex, was sacralized; struggle to transcend or overcome enemies of Yahweh, not the search for ecstatic union, was the mode of salvation. The practical effect of this concept of God's self-revelation in historical acts, in the building of the holy city and the kingdom, was the desacralization of sex and nature for the Hebrews.

But this, of course, does not mean that the Hebrew tradition considered sex to be profane or evil or especially pervaded by sinfulness. The positive attitudes toward sex of Genesis, the Song of Songs, and the Book of Hosea are well-known. For the Hebrews sexuality was a *human* matter, to be regulated for practical and political necessities, but not a religious reality with absolute value or disvalue. The human experience of sexual love was seen to be natural and good, and a matter of human responsibility. So it was that the new bride and groom were guaranteed a year together for special enjoyment. The man, even the king, who sent a husband into battle so he could take liberties with the wife, was punished. Adultery was reprehensible and the spilling of seed was to be avoided because of the social importance of procreating the chosen people and of the orderly distribution of property. One acted responsibly in one's sexual life, but sexual activity was not an imitation of God's activity for there was nothing in the concept of Yahweh to serve as a model for this aspect of created life. Sex was not God's affair, it was man's.

But then quite a new situation emerged as the developing community of Christ's followers struggled with the new concept of God that was revealed through Jesus. In Jesus the Christ there is a God who is a model for human life!

In the Father, Christ, and the Spirit, there is a God who is in dynamic interpersonal relation. The Old Testament used sexual images, but its basic purpose was religious: to tell something about God. The New Testament gradually developed a religious language whose basic purpose was existential: to reveal something about human life. For Christians' understanding of sex the result was ambiguous. On the one hand a devotion to the imitation of Christ may be patterned after his martyrdom and may find its fulfillment in bodily asceticism and abstinence from sexual relations. Such abstinence was not an imitation of Jesus' own sexual abstinence; rather, it was based upon a theological view of the "end time" and the passing away of all temporal concerns. Nonetheless, it produced a spirituality in which the highest goal was thought to be a life without sex in imitation of a sexless Christ and a sexless God. The injunction in 1 Corinthians 7:1, "It is good for a man not to touch a woman," might be the first written evidence of Christian asceticism.

On the other hand there is a baptismal and marital theology in the epistles attributed to Paul that, in effect, resacralized the sexuality of Christians. In such passages as " . . . in all that you do, whether you work or play, do all in the name of the Lord

Jesus" and "this is the great mystery; in the love of a man and woman is the love of Christ for his church" the resacralization of natural life takes place. It is said that the great passage from Galatians 3, "In Christ there is neither Jew nor Gentile, slave nor free, male nor female," is a baptismal formula that reflects the conviction, shared by the early Christians, that Christian existence transcends the cultural world, including its sexual distinctions. For some this transcendence meant the freedom to do any sexual act, like the man who married his stepmother; for others it meant rejection of all sexual acts. Even in these early times there was wide variation in behavior among groups of Christians and a variety of beginning theologies of how one should live who had in effect entered into the resurrection with the Lord Jesus.

Although the theologizing that these passages call for—on sexual love as the sanctifying symbol of marriage—did not take hold until the twentieth century, the church did accept, in practice, the sacramentality of marriage. More important than the sanctity of sexual love, however, was fidelity (that is, a lifelong, exclusive relationship) and parenthood (that is, the procreation and education of children).

Consciousness of the sacredness of sex seems to be a fragile thing indeed. It appears to emerge in brief periods of insight only to be overwhelmed once more by asceticisms and philosophies hostile to the body.

The danger confronting our contemporary age with regard to the human experience of meaning in sexual life seems to be just the opposite of the threat apparent to the great prophets of Israel. Then the religious meaning assigned to sex was so numinous that it endangered—or seemed to endanger—the singleness of devotion exacted by Yahweh from the covenanted people. In our time, sexuality has been so completely desacralized that it is in danger of being depersonalized. There is no mystery, no union, expected by many people for whom sex is no more than release of tensions and a few minutes of closeness with one other warm body. Christians can discover a message that may help people today to find the meaning that is *already there*. This message is not: "transcend this—avoid this—use this unholy thing only as a means to the holy thing of childbearing," but rather: "Expect connecting love to be holy love. Expect to find here the experience of that Other who calls you out of yourself to love and to relationship and to a creative task in society. Know that your bodies, even as they symbolize or make present your person, also symbolize God. And where you make his love present, God is present and active."

What are some practical effects of taking seriously the sacramental character of our capacity for sexual love?

First, with a sacramental reality all the difference is made by the *meaning* that is perceived. Moreover, it's a kind of meaning that cannot be conveyed in words, but one into which one is initiated experientially. I think one of the reasons that sex is so rarely a religious experience is because the sex education Christian children receive is so rarely a religious formation in self-esteem, reverence for the other as already loved, and an experience of the Christian community as a place of expansion and growth of life.

Second, to recover the insight that our sexual lives and our spiritual lives are not mutually exclusive should not lead us to discard the wisdom that resides in our tradition—whether in its preventive morality or in its practical leniency. But we should have the courage to apply a corrective. Pride and exploitation constitute the biblical notion of sin and are the proper theological definition of concupiscence. Erotic passion or the pleasure drive or the abandon that characterizes the ecstasy of sexual climax is not accurately represented by the category "concupiscence."

Third, sacramental realities are as open to abuse in their natural symbolism as all other realities are. But the possibilities of abuse—in this case, the demonic element of sex—should not be used as a reason for avoiding them altogether, or for constructing an image of redemption and grace that exclude them. They are no more or less dangerous and destructive than food, that other symbol of union that human beings also experience in its demonic properties. The insight of the Old Testament is that sex is not demonic but human; the insight of the New Testament is that faithful, relational sex is sacramental.

Fourth, when the sacramental attitude toward sexual expression replaces the presupposition that sexuality is best left unexpressed, then the Christian has a different obligation. The virtue is not in repressing but in cultivating the human capacity to respond sexually. While extremely significant, this aspect of personal development is not altogether different from intellectual, physical, or spiritual development. One does not come into life fully developed; one has an obligation to grow toward full adulthood. The Christian community shares the responsibility of preparing its members for the fullest possible expression of intimacy and love. Love, after all, is the greatest of the gifts of the Spirit, and the Incarnation remains the central mystery of our faith.

Abraham Maslow, speaking of love and sexuality in "self-actualizing people" characterized their sexuality as follows:

• They enjoy genital sex wholeheartedly, *far above* average, yet specific sex acts or goals do not play any central role in their lives.

• Sex itself may bring on mystical experience at times, yet at other times is simply experienced as lighthearted and playful.

• Their talk about sex is considerably more free, casual, and unconventional than the average.

• They are aware of their sexual attractiveness but are less driven to secretive affairs precisely because their own sexual partnerships are profoundly satisfying.

• They make no sharp differentiation between the roles and personalities of the two genders. They are so certain of their maleness or femaleness that it is no threat to them to take on some cultural aspects of the opposite sex role.

• Their love relationships are characterized by elation, merriment, a feeling of well-being, gaiety.

• They affirm the other's individuality, are eager for the growth of the other, respect the other's unique personality.

While posed in psychological language, this is a remarkable portrait of grace and freedom at work in an individual. These people are so, says Maslow, because their needs have already been met: they have been loved and are thus free to love in response. Grace, according to Saint John, is experienced in that one has first been loved by God and knows that love in Christ and the community. Reclaiming the graced meaning of sexual love could give new meaning to the impression made by some of the early Christians: "See how they love one another!" It is not sexual activity in itself that is scandalous, but precisely that Christians have come to be characterized in the popular mentality as repressed, rigid, legalistic, and incapable of responding humanly to a human need or situation.

Fifth and last, the understanding of what constitutes religious experience—prayer—needs to be reformulated to include the sexual aspects of life. Images of prayer and meditation have come through a monastic tradition that is inseparable from its historical ideal of sexual abstinence. But God's presence is known by the *effects* in one's life of the encounter with the sacred. We might say that wherever one is given a new beginning, wherever something is made real or realized in a new way, wherever that happens, the reality of God has been present to us. If God can only be found where God is supposed to be—in the churches or in the present order of things—then there is no mystery left, and not even the churches are sacramental. God's free and ever outpouring love finds its way through every seam and crack in our personal universes. The false dichotomies between body and spirit, sexuality and sacredness, cannot remain unchallenged.

2·

Friday: Sweeping the House
Social Science and Sex Research

A presupposition of the primitive world was that divine reality broke into the human being's experience through natural things that remained natural. One learned about God from a stone, let us say, not by looking *past* it, but by understanding and revering its stoniness. Likewise, in order to appreciate the revelation about human life that God intends to make through sexuality, our first task is *not* to look past it to what the Bible, the church, or various ideologies have supposed to be true about it. The first task is to appreciate it by knowing as much as possible about it in itself. This is partly an experiential mode of knowing, but experience cannot be communicated until it has been formulated in language. The accumulation of findings about human beings living their sexual lives is most usefully available to us today through the data and information of the empirical and social sciences. Only by knowing what sex says about itself in human lives will we know what God reveals through it and what it reveals about God.

Therefore, the supernatural perspective, to be truly authentic, must start by asking the natural question. What is the best of contemporary information on the anatomy and physiology of sex? What are its implications for theology and ethics?

Traditional Christian teaching about sex was based upon the scientific knowledge available at the time of its formulation.

Present-day Christian teachers have too often repeated and reinforced the *conclusions* of their distinguished forebears without
looking at the premises, at what was assumed to be fact. Many of
those premises have been invalidated by subsequent observation
and research; the conclusions which they supported should have
been rejected. But since those conclusions have been legitimized
by ecclesiastical authority and tradition, they often have sur-
vived much longer than their foundations warranted.

The intent of this chapter is to imitate the great teachers in
their methods rather than to repeat their conclusions. It will be a
sketchy and selective discussion, but more detailed information
cannot and need not be repeated here.[1] Enough will be repeated,
however, to make the point that we must consult the empirical
and social sciences in order to discover the meaning of natural
reality as it functions as a vehicle for the sacred. One does not do
theology *over against* the facts, but builds upon them.

What then are the facts about sex that have come to light in
the twentieth century? What are the implications of these facts
for the religious meanings and moral values attached to sex in
the minds of contemporary people?

In the first place, much of what had been considered "natural"
in sexual custom and practice has been shown to be the result of
cultural, social, political, and historical variables. We now know
that the biological givens are just one small part of human sexuality: to analyze the physical organs and the reproductive cycle
is not yet to understand the nature of human sexual desire and
practice. In fact, what God has given us, in the sexual as in all
other spheres, is not a completed nature, but the ability to learn
(and become) from experience. Our sexual experience is in part
the product of the nurturing that takes place from early childhood and that assigns certain names and meanings to bodily
movements and personal feelings.

Experiments with animals have shown that if they do not learn
when young how to initiate or respond to an encounter with the
opposite sex, they are not able to function sexually as adults and

often either are unable to complete the sexual act or engage in violent and inappropriately aggressive behavior. The effect of social isolation in infancy on adult sociosexual behavior can be calamitous. In one experiment deprived males were visibly aroused in the presence of females but stood by puzzled, not knowing what to do. Either they groped aimlessly and acted clumsily with receptive females, or they brutally assaulted them. Females who had been in social isolation mistrusted physical contact and either fled or attacked the males. They could, however, be induced in time to tolerate at least some sexual contact with undeprived males.

Although we cannot and should not attempt to test these findings on humans, they suggest much that is true of inadequate human sexual development. These experiments leave no doubt that heterosexual activity develops adequately only where there is affection. Even the postures and feelings characteristic of coitus have to develop in the play and interactions of infancy and childhood.

Because of the greater development of the human brain human interactions are infinitely more complex than those of animals, which makes the implications of deprivation much more serious: neither "nature" nor instinct teaches us how to achieve mature sexual love. The development of that ability involves trust, acceptance of physical contact, and motivation. The body's chemistry may produce sexual arousal and genital sensation, but human sexual experience is only produced by social and personal sensitivity.

The ability to love sexually for a human being is, then, *made*, not born. The importance of this fact can hardly be overestimated. The ancient idea that the only proper human response to one's own sexuality is to control, inhibit, and restrain it must be modified by the realization that, like any other human faculty, sexuality depends for its proper use on experience and cultivation. Full and satisfying intimacy is learned. It is more than a small part of the central glory and obligation of human living, the ability to love. Moreover, if intimacy is part of full humanity, then each individual has a fundamental right to education that would facilitate the cultivation of this ability to its highest potential. The practical application of this principle and its implications will become clear when we consider our social obligations to provide appropriate initiation into sexual knowledge for young people, to celebrate ritually points of passage from one mode of sexual existence into another (for example, from singleness to partnership or from marriage to life without a partner), and to communicate an image of handicapped or disabled persons that includes the freedom to explore meanings and techniques of sexual love within their life circumstances.

When human sexual behavior was thought of as "innate" or as a "drive," the response of society was to build a few fences, get out of its way, and hope for the best. The religious image that this approach fostered was of a "bestial" or "demonic" power that worked its way in our bodies and could only be contained by celibacy or marriage. The image implies an alienation of sexuality from personality: sex was an "it" that sought to dominate the "I." Obviously, the long history of an alienated sense of the body needs to be brought to a close, not just because the social fruits of such dualism are so frightful—sexism, racism, classism—but because it is based on a fallacious theory. What was thought to be instinctive and completely biological is in fact the product of conditioning, even though it has been conditioning largely by neglect, circumstance, and, perhaps, political expedience. Knowledge that our sexual behavior is learned, even though we cannot unravel all the factors that are involved in that learning process, has left us freer than ever before in history to form persons who know how to love, and how to love sexually with a wholeness in which body and spirit are not pitted against each other. This is why sex education, as a powerful tool in the cultivation of our faculties for love and union, today belongs within religious education or, better, in that category known more popularly as "spirituality."

Modern sex research has also shown that human sexual behavior is extremely varied. What is actually done by people from their youth to their old age is very different from popular expectations. This variety, with the numerous descriptive reports that detail it, has striking implications for those who would prescribe a kind of sexual behavior that is "natural," "normal," and to be accepted in a particular society. Of course, modern statistical studies have limitations that must be kept in mind when formulating specific conclusions from any one of them, but their great strength is that they derive from real experiences of real people. One of the psychological benefits for the individual who knows their findings is the opportunity to put one's own anxiety, guilt, and fear in perspective. "Is this normal? Am I normal?" are the great torturing questions of adolescents beginning to feel the movements of sexual response. According to Kinsey, the only unnatural act is one you can't do; according to Albert Ellis, "normal sex behavior is anything and everything that we — or that the societies in which we happen to live — declare and make it to be."

Of course, the points made earlier remain true. Each human being is born into an already constituted society and his or her nature is "made" according to the images and rituals of the society. Some forms of behavior are acceptable simply because customs or laws make them statistically normal. Until very recently, the woman who would initiate a date, a marriage, or sexual intercourse was a statistical abnormality. When attitudes change, the statistics change, and so does the "normality" of the act.

Another criterion of what is normal has been biology, or better, human interpretations of their biological organs. The clearest example is the notion that the only purpose of sexual organs is heterosexual intercourse and that the only purpose of intercourse is reproduction. If that were true, it would follow that only procreative sex is normal.

A third criterion used by societies to judge the normality of sexual behavior is its effects on the person: that which makes us feel healthy, happy, and emotionally and physically fulfilled is normal; that which frustrates us or makes us feel anxious and tense is abnormal. The most typical example here is self-pleasuring. But of course, positive as well as negative attitudes are taught. To appreciate that fact, one need only watch the parents of a toddler preparing the child for Christmas. "Oh, look! Isn't it pretty," they say. "You're going to get presents, and the tree will be so beautiful. Don't you just love Christmas?" Then, when the child coos with pleasure on Christmas morning and says, "I just *love* Christmas," they seem surprised and attribute it to some innate affinity between the innocence of childhood and the Christmas season. Many children are still taught by silence, embarrassment, and negative looks that exploration of their own bodies is dirty and abnormal. The sad thing is that such categorization does not prevent the behavior, but only serves to surround it with secrecy and guilt and to render all pleasure somehow suspect.

Finally, the kinds of behavior that a society judges to be moral may become for that society the standard of what is normal. All too often, however, such standards endure largely because the members of the society who do what is considered immoral cannot admit it openly and must either leave the society or find a way of "beating the system" — usually by giving the appearance of living according to the society's moral standard, while, in fact, acting according to their own standards. The most readily recognized example is nonmarital sex. Statistically, nonmarital sex may not be abnormal at all.

The point of this discussion is that the social sciences have begun to develop an instrument through which we may in fact come to discover what people actually *do* in an area of life that has been hidden in shameful secrecy or distorted by allegedly humorous "conquest" talk. In order to evaluate human sexual behavior, we must take into account the whole range and variety that it in fact exhibits. When the only admissible evidence is that which has been determined as normal at the outset, we deprive ourselves of data that are necessary. We then spend our energies on protecting a hypocritical image: an "ideal" world in which image is more important than reality, and an underworld in which there is no possibility of transcending that brutal reality.

Sex research has shown that sexual fantasies are the most

universal of all sexual behaviors. From self-pleasuring and erotic dreams, kissing and exploring, oral-genital sex and intercourse to variations that are less common and less understood, the human race has shown no less variety and creativity in its sex life than in its development of languages, cuisines, arts, and cultures. What is different is that there has been in the past neither communication nor celebration of this variety in human sexuality. Because of historical accidents or the needs of particular social forms, we have profaned sex while humanizing food, art, and language. Sexual variety was most often not known; when it appeared it was explained through polarizing teminology like "us/them," "evil/good," "pagan/Christian," "animal/human." The amount of objective data we now have about human sexual behavior puts a grave responsibility on religious thinkers and writers. Before they come to their conclusions, they must return to the experience of people and consider the empirical evidence. As they would not construct a building without consulting architects and contractors, so they must not construct an ethic or define sexual realities as entailing sin or grace without consulting the best scientific writing on sex.

As Teilhard de Chardin said, the primary sexual organ of the human being is the brain. Humans do not have an estrus cycle similar to that of many animals who are interested in sex only when the female is ovulating and capable of being impregnated. Most higher animals are in heat only during certain times of the year, and only then are the females receptive to intercourse. Human beings, by contrast, are capable of sexual intercourse whether or not the woman is capable of becoming pregnant. This is extremely significant, for it challenges all those dualistic notions that sex belongs to the body and spirit belongs to the mind. Human beings, precisely in their sexuality, *least* resemble the animals, for human beings are freed, sexually, from the demands of the reproductive cycle. There is even some evidence that the woman's desire is greatest precisely at that time at which she is least likely to conceive. Why have animals, in which the estrus cycle and instinct predominate, been used in the past as data to determine what is natural for human beings? The answer is, of course, that ancient thinkers relied on the ethology of their own times and assumed that human beings in their bodiliness and sexuality were more like animals than different from them. Given imperfect observation techniques and very limited samples, the conclusions that were drawn about the natural end of sex being procreation seemed logical and irrefutable.[2]

Moreover, female anatomy indicates that pleasure and play are as much nature's purpose for sex as reproduction. Not only is it clear that the sexual capacity of the human female is separate from her reproductive cycle and controlled by her brain, but it is also clear from the presence of the clitoris that nature intends pleasure, at least for the female, to be separable from procreation. This small pea-size organ, hidden by a hoodlike fold of the labia, has absolutely no function with regard to conception or birth, yet, it is the source of the most intense pleasure. If the Creator—if nature—does not intend such pleasure, then one would have to regard this phenomenon as a mistake—a rather arrogant position for those who take pride in having discovered human law from observation of nature. One response to the discovery of something in nature that contradicts one's ideology is to imply, if not assert, that something other than God is responsible for this "aberration" and to attempt to rectify the situation. As we will see, there has been no lack of such theories. Dualistic systems of philosophy and religion have speculated that the source of the female body is the devil or a prinicple of evil, or that it is the result of sin. Needless to say, this is heretical and blasphemous in a religious world view in which one God, creator of all, is worshiped and glorified.

Some societies, particularly those where women are regarded as chattels, practice a kind of circumcision of females in which the clitoris and parts of the labia minora are removed. It is widely practiced in eastern, western, and central Africa, as well as in some parts of Brazil, Malaya, Pakistan, Egypt, and among a

Christian sect in the Soviet Union. In El Salvador, it is still not uncommon for a mother to carve the sign of the cross with a razor across her daughter's clitoris. In the United States and England, it was practiced occasionally during the nineteenth century as a means of curtailing excessive sexual desire in women. The purpose of such genital mutilation is to curb what is thought to be the excessively sexual nature of women. Female circumcision is, therefore, quite different from male circumcision (also a genital mutilation and often justified on religious grounds) in that it virtually eliminates a woman's human capacity for sexual pleasure. As a political act, it controls and curtails her humanity in a most intimate area. By contrast, male circumcision does not interfere with sexual functioning or pleasure in any way, but seems simply to facilitate cleanliness.

Obviously, clitoridectomy is not practiced on contemporary American women, but there is a psychological and spiritual mutilation that prevails. The fact that the clitoris as a gift of God is denied by those who fear that its power for self-pleasuring and fantasy will lead to infidelity and to the breaking up of homes, as well as by those masses of women who are so far from owning their own bodies and personalities that they do not even know what they have "down there."

How can we account for the fact that the clitoris, with its orientation to pleasure, has been ignored while the uterus and penis, with their orientation toward procreation, have been used as a model for natural law? It may be because so much of the "thinking from experience," which characterizes philosophy and theology, was done from *male* experience and male sexuality. Women's sexuality was surrounded by the secrecy of "women's rites" and since only men were educated sufficiently to be the writers and researchers, facts about female anatomy, physiology, and response were inaccessible. Even if accessible, such facts would have been considered inadmissible because, according to theories of fetal development accepted in the past, the conception of a female was thought to be an accident due to defective sperm or the presence of unfavorable conditions, such as a humid breeze at the time of conception. Since male characteristics were considered normatively human, it is no wonder that the "unique" characteristics of the female were considered at best irrelevant and at worst an aberration to be corrected.[3] Nor is it surprising that the clitoris and its function escaped notice for so long. Who would expect the church fathers to take it into account when many women themselves continue to be unaware of its existence?

The existence of the clitoris in the female provides a natural basis for the development of a theology of mutual pleasure and play in human sexual experience. Its implications for fullest development of human potential are obvious and compelling, especially at a time when women, along with other marginal groups, are pressing their claims to such development.

Sexuality pervades evey aspect of personality and life. It is not simply a matter of the genitals, nor a necessary evil, nor an optional accessory, but a constitutive element of the human being. Learning to be a human being involves learning to be a man or a woman and learning how to express and respond to human love in a physical way. When sex was seen to be an "add-on," whether as a result of sin or for purposes of procreation, it made sense to ignore or inhibit it during menstruation, before marriage, after menopause, and if one is widowed, divorced, handicapped, retarded, or for any reason not able to establish a family. If sexuality is expendable and a kind of "luxury" the weak cannot do without, then celibacy and continence as tests of spiritual strength make some sense. But if it is crucial to human personal awakening and interpersonal relationships, then increased reverence and careful education toward its responsible use are required of everyone.

Less than ten percent of American children receive any kind of formal sex education, even though evidence shows less premarital pregnancy and fewer divorces among those who do. For these seven percent or so, sex education is largely reproduction education. They are given information on male and female "plumbing" and the stages of fetal development. There is little discussion of relationship and responsibility. Because public-school education still intends to be "value free," and because private schools are often controlled by religious and parental groups that want to keep their children's education "sex free," the integration of one's actual sexual life into the rest of life suffers greatly. One of the results is a kind of schizophrenia between expressed morals or values and personal acts. Examples abound: Rape is the fastest growing crime in America. A 1974 study says that ninety percent of women under twenty-five have had premarital intercourse. By age sixteen, one in five has engaged in coitus; by age nineteen, two out of three have done so, and more than nine out of ten have had sex prior to marriage. It is not beside the point, of course, that social conditions producing late marriages, along with early puberty and sex-stimulating media, help to produce such statistics.

Masturbation, or better, self-pleasuring to orgasm, is another area in which the contradiction between openly held values and private action can create problems of guilt and anxiety. Ninety-five percent of males are said to masturbate to the point of orgasm during adolescence, with declining incidence after that time; many men continue, however, even through years of marriage. Female statistics are low during adolescence; girls seem to begin later than boys, but eventually the same percentage of males and females use some form of self-pleasuring to orgasm. The social concern of the past over the perceived problem of child and adolescent masturbation has not seemed to have had positive effects. Negative effects include denial, secrecy, guilt, and the continued identification of pleasure with evil.

Fifty percent of the total sexual outlet of American males is obtained through socially disapproved or even illegal means. Among single, divorced, and widowed men, the incidence of coitus and other sexual activity so obtained is well over ninety percent. Less than twenty percent of sexually active girls practice contraception. In 1980, there were one million teenage pregnancies in the United States; six hundred thousand teen-agers gave birth, thirteen thousand of them were girls under the age of fourteen. (At the same time, from eighty to ninety percent of Catholic women of childbearing age use some method of "artificial" birth control, despite papal condemnation. The fastest growing method of contraception is, in fact, sterilization.) When asked why they didn't protect themselves beforehand rather than risk pregnancy, some girls answered that they didn't want to seem as though they had *planned* it. But in a truly integrated human life, the most crucial decisions, of which sexual decisions rank very high, ought above all to be conscious, considered, and planned.

The average life span of persons in contemporary society has increased dramatically. Today the average life span is seventy-four years, compared to forty-seven in 1900, and eighty-four is projected for the year 2010. A longer life, of course, means much more than just additional years. It involves a whole network of new relationships, from the heterosexual friendships that characterize our extended adolescence to the work partnerships of men and women in their professional or wage-earning capacity to unprecedented relationships with and among the aging and the aged. Now that reliable methods of conception control have made marriage separable from sex and sex separable from the family, new meanings and structures for the contents of a full human life are required. In marriage itself, the formula "so long as we both shall live" represents a far different burden when that period is likely to be sixty rather than twenty years, and when it can include forty or more years after children are grown.

Genetic research and reproduction technology is already creating new possibilities and problems. It is possible to determine the gender of a child, to manipulate heredity, to initiate the growth of a fetus outside the womb. The number of possibilities, along with decisions to be made on individual and global levels, continues to grow. The great problem will be to relate the basic values of life, freedom, creativity, reason, and love to the concrete choices of the present. The Judeo-Christian tradition, at least in its past formulations, does not contain the answers to the personal dilemmas we will face. As Richard A. McCormick notes,

> In this sense I believe it is true to say that the Judeo-Christian tradition is much more a value raiser than an answer giver. And it affects our values at the spontaneous, prethematic level. One of the values inherent in its incarnational ethos is an affirmation of the goodness of persons and all about them—including their reasoning and thought processes. The Judeo-Christian tradition refuses to bypass or supplant human deliberation and hard work in developing ethical protocols within a profession. For that would be blasphemous of the word of God become human. On the contrary, it asserts their need, but constantly reminds people that what God did and intends for us is an affirmation of the human and therefore must remain the measure of what persons may reasonably decide to do to and for themselves.[4]

Codes of ethics regarding the human use of sex have only very limited usefulness if they do not take into account the meaning of its integration into life. A guide that is realistic does not engender hypocrisy and double standards. The facts seem to show that most human beings do not regulate their sex lives formally and with clearly acknowledged intent. They seem to be less than open-eyed about it. At best, we have general, prethematic feelings about how we should behave sexually. Most of us conform out of inertia or fear, and when we break rules, we do so mainly on impulse. The kind of decisions made under such pressures of the moment are usually compromises which we cannot justify later; the consequence is a growing complex of guilt that, psychologists tell us, provides the energy for the repetition of just those unacceptable, compromising acts.

A more adequate understanding of both sexuality and religion would, however, make it clear that there are good religious reasons for having sex, not just for avoiding it. And there are good religious reasons for preparing oneself positively for a life of physical and personal intimacy. In practically all instances, psychogenic sexual dysfunction (such as impotence and frigidity) could have been circumvented had the individual received a positive, well-timed sex education. Fear of failure underlies most sexual malfunction, with the next most common cause being religious teachings and the guilt and anger they engendered. But sexual incompetence is not innocence: any adult who enters a relationship with a legitimate expectation of sexual partnership is doing her partner an injustice if she cannot act effectively to produce sexual union and the human joy that accompanies its loving expression. It is simply not true that we do no wrong sexually if we do nothing at all. Positive preparation for a mature life of love must permit the growth of intimacy while at the same time instilling the restraints necessary for social living. A well-balanced Christian attitude must include *incentives* as well as *prohibitions* for human sexual integration.

It should, of course, go without saying that the use of others sexually to vent frustration or to gain some degree of physical relief and pleasure is *not* what is meant by human sexuality. This is a difference of kind and not just of degree. When adults (usually, according to statistics, heterosexual males) use children or very young prostitutes, they are abusing their own sexuality as well as the person of the other. Such acts are truly profane and have nothing to do with relationships that strive for interpersonal intimacy and growth, even though such an adult may think, as sex offenders often do, that the other "likes" it and is not being hurt, in fact is even benefiting by it and being paid. This is exploitation at its worst, for the sacredness and the significance of the sexuality of the child-woman (or boy) is being violated before she is able to come into full and human possession of her own body.

The existence, and what appears to be the increasing frequency, of adult/child sex does not invalidate the call for a positive recognition of the sacredness of sexual love. Rape is not sexual love. It is the use of another by physical or psychological force.

This is violence, not human sexuality, though the genital organ may be the weapon used. The other in such a situation is a powerless object, perhaps fearful and confused, but certainly not a free subject willing to express mutual and personal love. Unfortunately, our legal institutions and even our churches have failed to express the kind of outrage that this desecration of others deserves. Such failure is likely related to the general fear of dealing with matters that are sexual and the general reluctance to affirm the sacredness of the sexuality of each human being.[5]

By contrast, to cherish sexuality as a sacred vehicle of relationship to God and to others would lead to absolute rejection of the use of others — children, women, or men — for experimentation and exploitation. The atmosphere of permissiveness and denial that now prevails has *not* resulted from our cherishing sexuality too dearly. The abuses of sex with which the media bombard us should not close us, in shame and guilt, to the celebration of human sex. Rather, a stronger sense of its sacred reality should enable us to denounce such abuses.

It is obvious that our theoretical knowledge of sexuality is considerably greater now than it was in biblical times. We now have new methods of acquiring knowledge, both descriptive and experimental. Moreover, we have new canons for evaluating old knowledge. We have historical and literary methods of evaluating biblical and historical sources to weigh their relevance for our decision making. The theological principle that grace builds on nature requires the use of the best contemporary knowledge. Christians affirm that God's self-revelation occurs through nature and in human history, and the better we know each of these the more likely we are to read God's revelation rightly. The religious assumption underlying the search for knowledge is that all truth is coherent with itself; the reasonable person who is at the same time a person of faith needs to listen closely and constantly for the word that actually is God's. Cautions are in order, of course. Research findings should be used as what they are — as descriptions of what appears to be the case in present human experience. They ought not to be taken as *prescriptive* of what human beings can or should do.

Users of research data must be aware of the presuppositions of the researchers. Unless these presuppositions about life, life's purpose, transcendence, and other crucial matters are raised to the level of consciousness and taken into account, they are likely to distort the work. One of the hazards of empirical science is the possibility that its practitioners are lured in to a dogmatically *reductionist* view of human being: the view that a person is *nothing but* his or her drives or *nothing but* a reflection of economic forces. It is important also to remember the cumulative character of all science: without critique and replication by equals in knowledge and skill, a theory remains weak and incredible. When verified in new experimental situations, it claims only probability, not certainty. When its adherents vastly outnumber its skeptics, the result is consensus, not necessarily truth. All human endeavor, including theology, is subject to history and limited by the partial view of human minds.

The way in which a question is asked determines to a certain extent the answer. When Kinsey and others used orgasm as the basic unit in determining frequency and variety of sexual outlets, they ended up with a distortion of sexuality. For purposes of quantification, sex was reduced to "orgasm." Anyone who assumes the studies to say that the only kind of human sex is orgasmic sex misunderstands the purpose of quantification; it was not to reduce the richness of human sexual expression to one of its components, but simply to find a way of discussing a multidimensional reality. Some studies of gay sexuality have been carried out by observation in bars and men's rooms. This choice of locale also has skewed the statistics, showing a greater degree of promiscuity than would have been evident if the research had been conducted in a different way. Responsible interpreters of such studies of human life must be able to identify the points at which the questions, the circumstances, the size of the samples, the places of observation, or the instruments of measurement affect the data.

The potential for the *abuse* of scientific data should not jeopardize their continued *use*. Practitioners should guard against abuse of the method or the data: the study of human experience is, as eveyone knows, extremely problematic, often unreliable, yet absolutely necessary for the question of human sexuality. *Life*, after all, is the test of good theory, including good moral theory; theory is *not* the test of life. Human existence and change is reflected in experience; abstract generalizations provide no mirror of growth.

The conflict between scientific findings about human sexual attitudes and behaviors and the tenets of official church teaching is a problem both for theology and for people in their daily lifes. The problem for theology is that of the norm by which truth can be evaluated. Is there another norm superior to that of science, an absolute norm that would test the findings of empirical science? Some say yes: that norm is revelation. Whatever does not agree with revelation is not true and must be rejected. Some say no: there is no positive norm of truth; there is only the negative norm that says: whatever is incompatible with the *whole of truth* cannot be accepted as true.

Revelation as a norm is problematic because revelation also comes to us in history, and we have only a partial and limited view, basically the view from the past, of what revelation permits and prohibits. The negative norm also is problematic because the test of inner coherence with all truth gives us little light. It may help us to discern *what cannot possibly be so*, but it cannot tell us *what is* so. One can live only by acting. Nonetheless, the responsibility of integrating new knowledge into old leads one to choose the second theological solution, that of the negative norm. When confronted with a new fact about human sexuality one accepts it as true according to the give and take of public discourse, unless it is absolutely incompatible with all that is held to be true.

As people hear religious voices repeating old laws and admonitions about matters such as masturbation and conception control—laws that are violated by the vast majority of the population—they are confused. Church teaching ought to operate at the level of principle and ought not to be applied insensitively to every person regardless of motive or circumstances. The fundamental principles remain unchanged and need to be affirmed in absolute terms: do good, avoid evil; respect life; love one another; forgive trespasses; be responsible. The rules or guidelines that are framed to help individuals in a given culture actualize those priciples and must be interpreted and applied with intelligence, love, and justice. When we look carefully at the best social science and the best well-reasoned theology, we may find more common ground than we would have guessed.

The following points are important. They are areas of consensus for almost all Christian moralists:

1. All human relationships have an incarnational character. They have a potential for unity that transcends individuals and reaches to society and to God.

2. The churches need a positive approach to sexual questions, one which would go beyond the repression of sins to the promotion of the positive values of sexuality.

3. The unitive or conjuctive meaning of sex is central. Married love cannot be seen merely as a means of procreation and education of children.

4. Men and women are fundamentally equal.

5. Persons caught in conflict situations deserve a compassionate pastoral approach rather than a condemning and judgmental one. This is based on respect for the conscience of each individual at each stage of his or her own spiritual development.

6. The reform of morals cannot take place without the reform of the social conditions of our society. Such reform must take place on the societal as well as the individual level.

7. We must develop methods of sex that both respect the primary responsibilities of parents and employ the best in current psychology, medicine, and theology.

Compared with these areas of agreement, the disagreements between science and theology, while serious, are relatively narrow. In fact, the disagreements do not touch the fundamental values of the Christian life. The disagreements have to do with how one should resolve certain conflict situations, such as sexual expression outside marriage, gay sex, conception control, and self-pleasuring.

What scientific studies about sex can tell us is that, given the chance, not everyone will experiment with every type of sexual behavior. Moreover, not every sexual behavior is equally healthy and life enriching. These studies also show that cultural differences endure and determine our attitudes to specific sexual behaviors.

The kinds of lives that human beings will fashion out of the mutually respectful dialogue between the scientific and religious perspectives on sex will be rooted in experience and produce self-esteem rather than compulsive guilt. Our ways of living our sexual lives will not be less demanding, but less rigid; not less helpful, but less prefabricated; not less moral, but less legalistic. In sexuality as in other areas, theology must consider all the evidence before drawing its conclusions. As Avery Dulles has pointed out, "Recognizing the stern demands of intellectual integrity, theology must pursue truth for its own sake no matter who may be inconvenienced by the discovery. Unless we are true to this vocation, we shall not help the church to live up to its calling to become, more than ever before, a zone of truth."[6]

3·

Saturday: Hiding the Treasure
Christian Teaching about Sex

Not many people are interested in the history of attitudes. Perhaps that is why the history of church teaching on sex is so little known. When we understand the *what* and the *why* of the past, however, there is likely to be a liberation of sorts. When the roots of a problem are revealed, we are freed to respond to it with greater clarity and objectivity. We are able to distinguish helpful from harmful factors and we are no longer in the unfortunate position of throwing away something before we understand its usefulness and then having to reconstruct it, painfully, again.

One purpose of historical reflection on Christian teaching about human sexuality is to serve the theological tradition. Loyalty to the tradition means to study it critically and lovingly, that is, with care, and thereby to enhance the tradition itself. This task is based on a view that sees the Christian tradition as ongoing and unfinished. The tradition is not a completed book, handed down intact. It is not a parcel of unchangeable propositions. It is rather a process of remembering a person. It is not a static thing, but a continuing action. In the handing down, there is also the responsibility for handing on, so while we receive the insights of past generations of Christians, we also reinterpret, refine, add, and cut.

Historical perspective is not a luxury; it is a necessity for theologians and teachers of historical religions such as Christianity. Likewise it is increasingly necessary for individual persons trying to live their lives according to Christian understandings. How else can one appreciate how one came to have certain attitudes toward sex? How else can we come to a clear decision about whether our attitudes are correct?

Theologians in recent years have alleged that certain aspects of Christian moral teaching on sex are contrary to, or in discontinuity with gospel living; psychologists have indicated that those teachings are often obstacles to the development of the fully human, fully actualized person. These two perspectives come together when one remembers Irenaeus's famous phrase: "The glory of God is man fully alive."[1] We pray for the glory of God with the words, "Thy kingdom come; thy will be done"; a part of this glory is men and women becoming fully human, fully developed in all aspects of their being. God's glory is diminished by any narrowed vision or truncated view of what it means to be a complete embodied person. If embodiment suggests temptation rather than empowerment, if our view of sexuality as a "bodily" characteristic is regarded as something that must be overcome and left unused while mind, will, and other spiritual faculties are to be developed, then our view of sex needs to be reexamined.

The fearful and negative judgment on sexuality that has often been part of Christian teaching is, in fact, an anomaly, and is inconsistent with other Christian doctrines. The church teaches the goodness of created nature in its doctrine of God as the sole creator of all that is. It affirms the goodness of human bodiliness, of life, and of history in its doctrines of the incarnation of God's Word as man and of Christ's bodily resurrection from the dead as a guarantee of the bodily resurrection of all. We celebrate the sacredness of matter in the eucharistic meal, where we communicate with God through the reality of Christ's presence in shared bread and wine. We even declare the equality in glory of woman with man by the doctrine of the bodily assumption of

Mary. But in the matter of sex, the tradition succumbed very early in its history to a negative view that associated sex with all that was gross and profane.

If such a negative view does not reflect the central Christian doctrines of creation, incarnation, and redemption, from where has it come? This question is increasingly important for historical theology, and while many early Christian writings are not yet accessible to students of religion, enough information has come to light to give us some new insights into the origins of Christian attitudes toward sex.

The story begins twenty-five hundred years ago with a shift in human consciousness that historians can describe and approximately date, but that they cannot explain. This axiological shift, one of three or four of similar significance in the history of humankind, took place somewhere between 600 and 200 B.C. and seems to have affected *every* religion of ancient times. Why it happened is still a puzzle, but what happened is quite clear. An attitude toward the earth and toward human life that has often been described as naturalistic but might more accurately be called sacramental gave way to a point of view that could best be described as "otherwordly." In all the religions of antiquity —Egyptian, Babylonian, Canaanite, Persian, Greek, Hebrew —the phase in which the earth, the body, fertility, sexuality, and woman's powers were celebrated as sacred gave way to an emphasis on transcendence, asceticism, the virile arts, building "the city," and attaining a better life after death. The natural cycles of life and love had been the privileged place for participating in divine creative power; now the goal of human life was seen as lying outside this bodily life, in another world and time and at odds with this world and this time. In this new view, God, the sacred, and divine creative power, could only be contacted by overcoming, or rising above, the earth, the body, and the sexual drive. Salvation, viewed as immortality of the spirit or disembodied soul, was the goal. Even the Hebrew Scriptures, so strong in the emphasis handed down from an earlier period on the unity of the living being, show evidence of this later debate about the existence of a part of the human being that might live on after death, and among the Hebrews ascetic groups emerged who went into the desert to live lives of self-denial.

The situation out of which Christianity developed was precisely this relatively new, otherworldly consciousness. There are some signs of tension between the two forms of consciousness even in the Gospel accounts. Jesus is accused of eating and drinking too much, and is misunderstood when he says "the kingdom of God is among you." The people's inability to see God in their midst troubled Jesus. (An old rabbinic tale summarizes the situation dramatically. Once upon a time, humanity decided to go in search of God, so it left its homeland and began to climb a very high mountain where, it was presumed, God could certainly be found. But just at the same time, the lonely God decided to come down the mountain to dwell at one with humanity. Unfortunately, they missed each other en route, and humanity ever since has been seeking unsuccessfully for God in those rarefied heights, while God remains present in the ordinary things of the earth.)

The unexplained shift from the sacredness of the here and now to the projecting of salvation into the beyond and the hereafter gave rise to an alienated experience of the body. The "I" now becomes an "it," a "thing" that stands between myself and my religious goal—that of being in relation to the center. The goal did not change. For mankind, real being always required being in relation to the sacred center. But now the sense of center shifted, and to get in touch with it one had to abandon what was now seen as profane and alien: the earth, the body—particularly the fertile female body—sexual bonding with all its intimacy and comfort and ecstasy. The classical Greek celebration of the body gave way to a Platonic flight from the body; the ancient cults of the earth mother gave way to religions of salvation of the disembodied soul after death.

Early Christianity drew upon these ideas at a time when all of them, including the Hebrew, were in their alienated, acosmic stage of development. This polarized experience of reality was expressed in a dualistic philosophy of being that perceived reality in terms of opposites — good and evil, spirit and matter, divine and animal, male and female — pitted against each other.

The importance of the contribution made by historical research is to show that it was *not* Hellenistic Christianity which was the source of the dualism that took over Christian thinking about sex. It was *not* Greek Christianity that vitiated the positive attitudes of Jewish Christianity. The shift toward dualism and fear of the body was a shift in consciousness that preceded Christianity and affected every ancient culture. It is possible to realize this in our time because, in the view of some observers, we are now in the midst of another shift of similar significance.

What this insight from historical research can do for us is to free us from certain dubious assumptions. We now realize that:

1. This dualistic attitude is *not* uniquely Christian and is therefore *not* endorsed by the words of Jesus or the guidance of the Holy Spirit.

2. Biblical statements regarding sex are *not* pure revelations of God's will and therefore are *not* normative for our lives and salvation.

3. There is *not* just one acceptable Christian view of sex.

Today it is clear that theologians need to reexamine the biblical materials in the light of the cultural context of biblical times and the shift of religious consciousness we know to have taken place. The Bible cannot be used without interpretation to tell people in the twentieth century what body, sex, and manhood or womanhood mean for us and require of us.

The early Christian church came out of the New Testament period (A.D. 50–120) with a few major concepts that continue to inform the tradition.

1. There is a common Christian concept of human life that values love as paramount.

2. There are specific condemnations of specific acts on spe-

cific grounds. It is clear in the epistles and in some Gospel passages that the writers intend to deal with particular situations, not to promulgate general principles that would be valid always and everywhere. When the specific grounds for condemnation shift, then, obviously, the condemnations are moot.

3. There is a resacralization of sexuality within marriage in the Letter to the Ephesians (5:21-32). Here the author shows sexual activity to be a grace-filled activity, reversing the desacralization of sex.

4. There is a clear statement of the Christian norm for marriage: as it was in the beginning—faithful, relational, lifelong (Matt. 19:3-12; it is interesting that Jesus does not emphasize procreation in this passage).

These concepts in no way reflect a negative view of sex, although the very lack of directly sexual information in the New Testament has led some commentators to regard it as disapproving of everything it does not explicitly endorse. This approach reads far more into the text—actually, into the text's omissions—than is appropriate to responsible interpretation.

Nonetheless, postbiblical teaching and practice of Christians became strongly and explicitly negative. Restraint, if not total abstinence, in the use of sex became the norm in the church of the second and third centuries. Some of the restraint can be explained by a theme that pervaded early Christian consciousness, the theme of the end of time. With the expectation that Jesus would come again, ending the world and heralding the Last Judgment, Christians, following sentiments of the Apostle Paul, were likely to say: "Why start something? The Lord is near and all this is to pass away." Neither family nor property makes sense when the individual future is thought to be dramatically brief.

Another factor was the desire of Christians to be like Jesus in his martyrdom and in his combat with the forces of evil.[2] It was thought at that time that one must live alone to struggle effectively with Satan and his power. This radical idea may explain why some people felt they must leave even the companionship of the city and go to the solitude of the desert to carry on their personal struggle against evil.

The only alternatives seem to have been marriage and virginity — virginity itself a kind of covenant marriage with God in which the soul was viewed as the bride. This, too, suggests that we are dealing with a society defined by marriage as the norm, marriage from an early age, either conjugal marriage or mystical marriage. This society simply did not deal with sexuality in the range of possibilities and life choices that is customary in our culture.

More research needs to be done into the motives behind the early Christians' decisions about sexual lifestyle. It appears to be the case that they, like us, imposed Christian motivations on decisions that had already been made on the basis of their contemporary scientific knowledge. One chooses, for example, to quit smoking, not for the love of God, but because of the health risks discerned by modern medicine. Nonetheless, we may find theological reasons to justify decisions made for reasons of health, or for what is thought at the time to be healthy. This is not hypocritical; in fact, Christians must do it. This is, once again, the sacramental principle. One knows what God wills and requires by examining, to the best of one's ability, the reasonable demands of nature and circumstances. Our ethics are based on conclusions drawn from the analysis of experience. What is good to do is good for the glory of God. Still, it is important to know when our decisions based on health and science have been overlaid with Christian motivation; when we know this, we will not religiously absolutize the content of such decisions. Saint Paul demonstrated that sort of awareness when he suggested that all remain unmarried, as he was; then he hastened to add, "I say this for your own benefit, not to lay any restraint upon you" (1 Cor. 7:25-39).

The early Christians were a radical sect with a unique vision of their community and its place in God's plan, yet they shared everyday assumptions about the human condition with others of their time and relied upon the philosophy and popular science of their age. The early Christians would not have expected to stand out from their contemporaries as having a unique view of the world, the necessities of a good life, or the meaning of happiness *any more than* American Christians today would expect to have a view of evolution, a standard of living, or an understanding of freedom not shared by their non-Christian counterparts.

One of the common assumptions in the second-century was that sex ought not to be highly valued as a necessity or a good in a full human life. Human life was defined within a dualistic view of nature. Of the two human components, the soul was thought to be more noble and true while the body, with all its complexity of movement, was thought more likely to lead to unhappiness and the loss of the fully human. This neo-Pythagorean view had had a long history, and even today is not without its adherents. But this theory did more than negate the body; it also identified maleness with the soul. The male (the soul) was rational, active, centered, right-handed, good; the female (the body) was irrational, passive, disorganized, left-handed, bad. The relationships of individual Christian men and women were certain to be affected by the inherent sexism of the current philosophy.

Another possible reason for the ethic of restraint that developed among Christians is found in their living conditions and social structures. Sociological factors were as important then as they are now in influencing what people do and how they think. A caution is in order, however: there was as much variety in the early Christians' living conditions as there was in their doctrines and we should not assume that they were a completely homogeneous group. Nonetheless, we can attempt to trace what became their typical approach with regard to sex without denying their variety.

During the first and early second centuries, Christians lived in what might be described as extremely close-knit communities. They were threatened with persecution; they were an underground church. It is easy to understand that they would have feared and avoided strangers, for strangers might betray them to the authorities. It has been observed elsewhere that groups which live in very close quarters for long periods of time develop sexual taboos. Perhaps the early Christians found it necessary strictly to control sexual relationships. Restraint, even abstinence, may have seemed the only way to protect their communities from the strain that the explosive pressures of sexual attraction, arousal, and jealousy might have produced.

But there is another possibility. As we know from early non-Christian writings, Christians were often accused of sexual license in their gatherings and liturgies. The Pauline letters contain evidence that some groups were, in fact, behaving in licentious ways that offended community standards. One group seems to have been so convinced of the resurrection of the body or so certain that the limits of the law were removed by baptism that they apparently lived in incestuous relationships. In Paul's response we find an example of a specifically Christian reason for adhering to the common morality of the times. Christians are to avoid certain forms of conduct, also considered immoral by non-Christians, because the bodies of Christians are temples of the Holy Spirit. The early Christians had to protect themselves from charges of sexual excess and this may have led to the severe limitation of sexual activity among their members.

What had been necessary at one point in their history to make Christians acceptable to their non-Christian fellows could very easily have become a trademark or special characteristic that eventually outlived its usefulness. The sociologist would say: what was adaptive became addictive. An insight from contemporary sociology of religion may throw light on this possibility as one of the sources of the Christian teaching regarding sexual restraint: marginal religions in America, especially those founded by women or encouraging broad participation by women, have tended to be extremely rigid and proper in their declared sexual standards. Similarly, some communities of primitive Christians appeared to control rigorously the behavior and relationships between women and men. It appears that the more revolutionary the doctrinal message of a new religious group, the more imperative it is that its moral standards be conservative in order for it to be accepted.

Whatever their living conditions, the goal of the early Christians was to live the life of charity that they understood to be mandated by the Gospel of Christ. We may have quite a different view of human nature, of the natural world, and of what makes for happiness, we may be in a vastly different social context, but our goal is the same: to live the life of charity mandated by the Gospel of Christ. Our way of living that goal, however, may prove to be quite different from theirs.

In the third and fourth centuries, a new mode of Christian teaching arose. No longer did it take place primarily through practical living and reflecting in community. Leadership was assumed by the more educated—by philosophers, lawyers, and physicians who emerged to formulate Christian teaching. If we are "buses in which our ancestors ride," the great thinkers of the second to the fifth century, the so-called fathers of the church, may be riding along in many of our attitudes toward sex. Justin, Irenaeus, and other Christian teachers affirmed the goodness of the original physical creation as a gift of God, but when they attempted to formulate the doctrine of redemption, a problem arose. How are we to be saved? What are we to be saved from? These questions came to be answered in a Platonic sense. We are to be saved by being freed from our gross material being to rise to our true spiritual (immaterial) being. It is easy to understand how Christian converts educated in Platonic philosophy should have attempted to understand and explain the faith in terms of that philosophy. This is inescapable. Even teachers today necessarily explain concepts, including salvation, in terms of their own contemporary world view.

Origen, a third-century theologian, was able to reconcile his belief in the goodness of all creation with a spiritualist view of redemption by formulating the process of redemption as the spiritualization of all creation. In his view, all of creation was originally, before the first sin, spiritually simple, a unity. Only after the Fall did it become gross, bodily, fragmented. Only after the Fall did mankind (Adam) become male and female. According to Origen, redemption is achieved for the individual through rejection of the flesh and through flight from material, sensuous nature. Origen, it is said, castrated himself in response to the Gospel saying about becoming a eunuch for the kingdom of heaven (Matt. 9:12).

Spiritualist assumptions were applied to gender as well. Maleness was identified with spirit; femaleness with matter, which is lower than spirit and must be transcended. This logic develops inexorably until Jerome can say that the more like a man a woman becomes, the closer she is to God. He held out the hope to female virgins that they could attain virility (i.e., become a *vir* ["male"] in Christ) if they lived their life of virginity faithfully. Jerome occasionally spoke lyrically about marriage, but only because he saw it as the social instrument capable of producing virgins for the Lord.

Given their philosophical background, it was impossible for these thinkers to conceive of God in terms of bodily, material, or sexual symbols. Even when they expressed a belief that matter was sacramental and that God was found in nature, they excluded the sexual and fleshly from this scheme. Hence they defined the image of God (Gen. 1:27) in the only terms they could: if man is made in the image of God, they reasoned, that image must be found in his spiritual nature, that is, in his soul as opposed to his body. This clearly implies that human sexuality represents something other than godlikeness. Some of the gnostics went so far as to characterize sex as an act of Satan; others more moderate saw it as part of animal nature. Whatever it was, for the thinkers of these ages it bore no resemblance to the divine.

Christianity by no means surrendered on all counts to the dualism of its time. The doctrines of creation and incarnation—and, to some extent, eucharistic theology and Mariology—were preached courageously, even though they were offensive to the gnostic groups that flourished everywhere from the second to the fourth century. Some of these groups and their antimarriage teachings were firmly declared heretical: Marcionism, which denied the place of the Old Testament in Christian Scriptures on the grounds that it was too earthly to have been inspired by God; Montanism, which went to extremes of self-denial and asceticism. In declaring these and other similar groups heretical, the church was giving testimony to its own sacramental sense that nature is good. By inserting the phrase "maker of heaven and earth" into the Apostles' Creed in the second century and by emphasizing the "Word was made flesh" in John's Gospel, the church was clearly struggling to affirm the goodness of creation and of human bodily being against the gnostic movement.

But it was not an easy battle. Particularly in the realm of sexuality, dualism triumphed.

Saint Augustine, born in 354 in a small town in North Africa, formulated more than any other early writer, the major ideas and established the terminology of the church's teaching regarding sex. He practically defined medieval theology, for his death coincided with the fall of many of the structures of ancient civilization and the response of Christian monks was to preserve the thinking of the fathers and teachers who had written before the movements of the barbarians changed the face of Europe and Christianity.

Augustine had two very strong passions—one for truth and one for sex. His *Confessions*, a personal journal, shows that he experienced these passions as mutually incompatible. His experience, however, may have been informed by the ideologies of the dualistic sects that flourished at his time. One of these sects was the Manichees, which Augustine joined as an associate member, an auditor, at the age of eighteen, asking them above all to teach him how to live a meaningful life. He remained with them for nine years and mastered their teaching, though he never mastered the discipline of life they prescribed. They taught that there is a cosmic struggle between good and evil (the two primal powers governing man), and that life is a constant struggle of flesh against spirit. Augustine was living with a woman at this time. It was not a formal marriage but a legal concubinage, a relationship recognized by Roman law. They had a son, named Deodatus ("given by God"). Even though the Manichees prescribed celibacy for their inner circle, Augustine was not able to break away from his family. He was plagued at the same time by a sense of guilt and degradation. Long before he became Christian, he was convinced that sex was a kind of bondage for a man, degrading but too strong to resist.[3] There is some evidence that he finally left his common-law wife in response to the nagging of his mother, who wanted him to marry a noblewoman. In any event, with his well-known conversion to Christianity, he, after one more brief liaison, renounced all consorting with females.

Augustine believed that sex had become a problem only after the Fall. He theorized that if Adam and Eve had remained together in paradise, there would have been no passion, no lust. The effects of sin appeared to him to be particularly present and powerful in the immoderate movements of pleasure and passion. Before the Fall, he speculated, Adam and Eve could have controlled their bodies entirely with their wills. His method of theologizing was apparently that of inductive reason: he observed that we can control our eyes, mouth, arms, and legs, but cannot control our genital organs. His view was based on the experience and observation of male sexuality, of course, and he came to the conclusion that the essence of sin is represented by the unruly penis, which refuses to follow the bidding of mind and will. Women are indicted by way of being the cause, occasion, and extension of this disobedience. Hence, women need to be controlled or avoided if sin is to be avoided.

This logic leaves something to be desired. It is the same logic that prevails when we are told that because men are likely to rape women, women should stay off the streets at night. But as Augustine observed his world and reflected on it, the argument seemed validated by the "innate" sense of shame that human beings display in covering the genital area.

The evil effects of the Fall, which resided particularly in sexual life, were theorized by Augustine to be passed on to new generations through intercourse. He assumed, as did everyone of his day, that only the material from the father was active in producing the child. In the act of intercourse, original sin was thought to be transmitted through the father's semen. But another theological problem comes up at this point: if sin is transmitted through intercourse, then Jesus, to be free of original sin, must have been the product of something other than human intercourse. It therefore appeared necessary for Jesus to have been born of a virgin and without the intervention of a human father in order to be considered sinless. Augustine developed the doctrine that original sin is closely related to sexuality, and added doctrinal support to the belief within popular piety that Jesus had no human father.[4]

From Augustine on, theological discussion of sex takes place *not* in the context of sacramental theology or theologies of creation or incarnation, but rather as a subcategory of original sin. What Augustine says openly—that intercourse is evil and responsible for passing on original sin—was modified and largely forgotten. But what he implies—that pleasure is degrading and sex is sin—has been remembered and circulates like a rootless weed. While Augustine resisted dualistic heresies and defended the faith on such issues as the true humanity of Jesus Christ and the omnificence of God, he succumbed to a negative interpretation of his experiences of sex that continues to influence us.

At the end of the fourth century there took place yet another development, unrelated to the thinking of Augustine but quite important for official Christian teaching about sex and its place in Christian life. Gradually, laws and customs arose that required eucharistic ministers—priests and bishops—to abstain from sexual intercourse before celebrating the eucharist. Normally, all priests and bishops would have been married (though bishops were expected to marry only once, and, if widowed, to remain continent thereafter) and the eucharist was usually celebrated once a week, on the Lord's Day. Such laws of abstinence were found in the Old Testament, although for the high priest it meant abstinence only once or twice a year. What happened at the end of the fourth century was that Christian communities in the West began to celebrate mass every day. What had been a reversion to Old Testament concepts of ritual purity became first a law of temporary abstinence while remaining in the married state, and then, because that was not enforceable, became a law of permanent abstinence, or celibacy.[5]

At the basis of the law of celibacy, which forbade parish priests to marry, was not the word of the Lord, nor a special charism given to an individual to live alone for the sake of the kingdom of God,[6] but the pre-Christian notion that the pollution of everyday life must be purged from the cultic leader before he can approach God. Foremost among the things that pollute men and women are contact with their bodies.

It is amazing to realize that underlying the law and practice of obligatory celibacy for the clergy is neither a spirituality nor a theology (that only came later), but simply a ritual taboo, a law of ritual purity that New Testament writers, especially Paul, insisted had been abrogated by Christ and was no longer binding on those who had been baptized in Christ. Celibacy as a requirement for clergy in the Roman Catholic church continues as a sign of the church's negative valuation of the body, of women, and of sex.

As the extant literature shows, the period from the sixth to the twelfth century in Christian Europe was not solely a record of asceticism and intolerance of sexual expression. Just as there was a pagan ascetic and antierotic tradition, so there was a Christian tradition of tolerant and positive attitudes toward love and eroticism. The monastic communities of men and women gave rise to a form of spiritual friendship, sometimes same sex but often heterosexual, in which the most tender and ecstatic sentiments were expressed in letters to each other. Writers like Ausonius, Sidonius, Apollinaris, Saint John Damascene, Marbod of Renne, and Saint Aelred of Rievaulx represent a minority voice, but one strongly in favor of an attitude toward sexual love characterized by delight in the good gifts of God.[7]

In medieval Christian literature there is much more discussion of marriage than of sexuality in general. Evidence survives in the form of marriage legislation and letters and manuals that were meant to guide the clergy in their pastoral work. Because marriage was considered a contract and a sacred thing—a sacrament —the church was more concerned with its purity (from impediments) and stability (free consent, love permanence) than with sexual excesses of the unmarried. According to Peter Lombard, those who sully a sacred thing by abusing it are punished more severely than those who habitually commit excesses. And the fault is more grievous in a married woman than in others. It is true . . . that a man who loves his wife too passionately is guilty of adultery.[8] Marriage was defended by the church on two fronts: from those who attacked it from the heretical position that chastity should be imposed on everyone,[9] and from those who sought to use it without regard for impediments, incestuous relationships, or the consent of the spouses. In fact, in the late eleventh century, the church won exclusive jurisdiction in medieval Europe over all matters pertaining to marriage, and marriage as a form of contract between feudal land-owning families declined.

From the fifth century, there had been a clear division between lay and ecclesiastical "orders." Separate codes of behavior required that the clergy "must not become subservient to the marriage bed" while the layman was expected to marry.[10] The endorsement of marriage, even for the layman, was not light-hearted, however; he was not to be prevented "provided he knew how to avoid lust, respected the times when sexual inter-

course was forbidden, and cultivated the fear of God and the
desire to beget children that would help him master the unruli-
ness of the flesh."[11] Married persons were clearly relegated to the
lowest rank of perfection, for marriage was basically a solution
of last resort. It was tolerated mainly as a remedy against "carnal lust." From before Augustine's time, the church recognized
marriage as a necessary institution because of its reproductive
function, but it was hard put to reconcile sex with a sacramental
sign of grace, for, as Odo of Cluny expressed it, the church saw
sexuality as the principal means by which the devil secured his
hold on creation. It was "better to marry than to burn," since all
sexual activity outside marriage was considered fornication,[12]
and all sexual activity within marriage had to be purged as much
as possible of pleasure and subordinated to the desire to procreate.

In order to endorse marriage without undue emphasis on its
physical rights and duties, the twelfth-century church-sponsored
model of marriage stressed the union of minds and hearts in
marriage, and especially emphasized the free consent or *dilectio*
("love") of the partners involved. In doing this, the church took
a stand, perhaps unintentionally, against the power of heads of
households to determine the marriage of their daughters and to
prevent the marriage of their younger sons or landless relatives.
It was the victory of individual choice over the social power of
the family, and, in this case, the church was the champion of
the individual's freedom to choose a spouse and to expect love in
marriage.[13] In this matter, the church also stood against male
supremacy, for it asserted the equality of the sexes in concluding
the marriage pact and in fulfilling the duties of conjugal life.

Saint Thomas Aquinas, the thirteenth-century theologian
who is considered the greatest of medieval thinkers, has been extremely influential in Christian thinking on matters of sex and
marriage and his importance for our analysis cannot be overestimated. Like Augustine, Thomas believed the highest human
good to reside in the life of reason and contemplation, but in

other ways he was very different from Augustine. He was free of the Manichaean influence that opposed flesh as evil to spirit as good. He was also free of a Platonic philosophy of being in which matter had no reality or value. Thomas built upon the philosophy of Aristotle, which was just beginning to be known and accepted in the West. Matter and bodiliness were not threats to salvation for Thomas, but the body, with its passions and enthusiasms, was troublesome insofar as it interfered with the serenity of the contemplative, that is, the good, life. Sex was an "inferior appetite" that, ideally, should be ruled by the intellect. But the pleasure associated with sex was not as great a problem for Thomas as it had been for Augustine. For Thomas, pleasure was the reward God associated with the good gifts he gave. Only at one moment, the moment of orgasm, did Thomas have a problem reconciling pleasure with the good and the humanizing because, according to Aristotle, at orgasm reason was momentarily blocked, and without reason there is no human act. A theology of ecstasy—that is, the transcending of reason—was possible for Thomas in his writing about prayer; at this stage of his understanding he could not envision a theology of ecstatic sex.

According to Augustine, intercourse, even within marriage, was sinful unless the following conditions were met: procreation (common to animals), mutual help to overcome concupiscence (unique to humans), and sacrament (reserved to Christians). Without these conditions, it was assumed that each act of intercourse was mortally sinful. Thomas accepted these goods of marriage, but he took the thinking farther. On principle, the good of the soul was always to be preferred to the good of the body; moreover, the good of the contemplative life was better than the good of the active life. On those bases, he developed a theology in which virginity and celibacy are affirmed as superior to the lay, or married, life.

Practical teaching regarding sex, although supposedly based on the laws of nature, became a complicated legalistic system that transformed the biblical "mystery" of loving one's spouse from a sacred and grace-filled act to a "rendering of the debt," a form of legalistic transfer of rights and duties. Although Thomas had developed many of the elements that might have produced a positive valuation of human sexuality, he was simply not able to do it. Only the duty of procreation saved sex from being sin. Far from viewing sex as a divine gift with which and because of which to praise God, sex remained a reminder of the Fall.

We must remember that these thinkers did not completely condemn the body or sex. Their position was rather one of strict cautions, restraints, and controls. The Christian virtues of courage and prudence were not invoked; rather, prevention and avoidance carried the day. And while these thinkers insisted on the ability of all creation to reveal God, and of human reason to hear God's message, their ideological dualism prevented them from seeing the inconsistency between their attitude toward creation and their attitude toward sex. Had they seen it, they might have worked the full implications of their sacramental and incarnational theology into their interpretations of sex.

After Thomas, things got even worse. During the Middle Ages, there was pluralism in theology. With their different points of view, schools, religious orders, and even political factions competed for a theological hearing. There were Franciscans, Dominicans, Augustinians, nominalists, realists, idealists. There was room for theological disputation. And in the everyday lives of people, there was room for divergence. Ordinarily, except for scholars, few people were aware of theological debates. Only at the point of requesting marriage in the church or taking vows in a community would they have made practical contact with canon law.

With the Reformation, Augustine's teaching achieved a new popularity. Some of the (admittedly slight) gains made for the value of pleasure in Thomas's teaching were lost or were subordinated to more pressing controversies. Devotion to Mary was challenged and with it the one symbol of the sacredness of womanhood that the church had celebrated. Many convents were closed, and with them vanished the one alternative that women had to subjugation by fathers, husbands, and sons.

With the Council of Trent, in the sixteenth century, the Roman Catholic church defined certain of its teachings more rigorously and established for the life of its clergy much narrower limits. The superiority of the life of virginity to marriage was authoritatively proclaimed. It now became possible to ask "What does the church teach about sex?" and receive a simple and definitive answer. Indeed, the catechism was developed to provide just such answers. Not "What does Thomas or Charles Borromeo say?" or "What do Christians in fact *do*," but "What is *official?*" Here the discussion of sex as an effect of original sin seemed to have been fixed forever.

Trent exhorted the faithful to avoid sex that was motivated by sensuality or pleasure and to abstain from rendering the "marriage debt" at least three days before receiving communion and often during Lent in order to devote themselves to prayer and meditation. It is not surprising that frequency of receiving communion dropped among the laity until it became necessary to legislate that all Catholics must receive communion at least once a year.

In our own time official church statements deplore sexual pleasure as dangerous and incompatible with the things of God. The priest is never to indulge, the unmarried laity never outside marriage, the gay or lesbian never, and the married not without openness to procreation. There have been changes in details, of course. The practice of rhythm for conception control had been denounced as a pagan hypocrisy by Augustine because the Manichees used it to prevent the entrapment of more souls in matter. Rhythm was, however, hesitantly approved by Pius XI in his encyclical *Casti Connubii,* and more positively by Pius XII. Since that time, "natural" family planning has come to be considered by the church as not only acceptable, but almost virtuous.

This chapter has given some sense of the sources out of which a largely negative view of sex has developed in the official teachings of the church. It has also shown some basis for valuing sex in marriage, fidelity, interpersonal love, equality of the sexes that are little known and little celebrated within the Christian tradition. The story is not yet finished. Christian experience and Christian thought are formulating new ways of expressing the reality of our physical potenial for love. A theology of sex that goes beyond mere rules and cautions is still being written.

4·

Sunday: Lighting the Lamp
A Social-Justice Context for Rethinking Sexuality

The argument of this chapter is that human sexuality, while of the greatest personal significance in its concrete expressions, is much more than personal. It is part of a social system that has until now been male-dominated. Its meanings — for men, and even more for women — have been confused by domination and submission, by exploitation and manipulation, and by the quest of some for control over others. The fact that these meanings are not essential to the bodily interaction between free and equal adults has largely escaped notice.

The context within which we live our lives — our "world," or our historical situation — affects the meaning of our sexuality. That meaning needs to be explored thoroughly before we presume to make or revise rules or guidelines. My purpose is not to write a sexual ethic, but to argue that the meaning of sexuality is essentially social and that sex is no less complex or capable of evolution than any other social question. Since ethical guidelines for behavior are invariably based upon the meanings and values that our actions are perceived to express, it is reasonable to expect that a new and more inclusive sexual ethic will become necessary.

In terms of values and meanings, sexuality is, at the present

50 |

time in this culture, most profoundly a question of power, and ought to be seen as such. The powerlessness of the female sexual partner has been eroticized through pornography and real or fantasized rape scenarios, and has been legitimated in religious writings through theological interpretations of the symbols of the "Fall" and the "headship" of the body. Female powerlessness has been regarded as "natural" to the relationship between male and female and has been taught as ordained by the "will of God." When seen for what it is — a question of power — it can be dealt with as a social reality open to evaluation rather than as an unchanging component of an absolute world view.

Every society has exercised some sort of regulation over such realities as food and sex. Such regulation has been necessary for the survival of the individual and for the stability and continuity of the group. From the beginning of recorded history there is evidence that the discovery had already been made that by disciplining sexual relationships rulers of a society could control the family. Such control served the stability of the governing power by regulating legitimacy, inheritance of property and titles, and population growth. Even so, some ancient societies (for example, in China, India, and the Near East) apparently interfered in matters *only* as they related to areas of public concern and only as much as was absolutely necessary. The morality of sex was the morality of human relationships in the group and for the good of the group. The potential it exercised for the survival, destruction, and ordering of society made sexuality a social matter.

It is also clear that the individual, under social constraints, most often used sex and marriage for social rather than personal purposes. Anecdotes to illustrate the point could easily be gathered from ancient as well as modern sources. Cicero, for example, had just divorced his wife, Terentia, and was asked whether he would marry again. "Certainly not," he replied. He "could not cope with philosophy and a wife at the same time." Almost at once, however, he was forced to retract. It had slipped his mind that he would have to repay Terentia's dowry and the only way he could raise the money was by marrying someone else. Although that incident took place a century before Christ, Cicero's situation is not so unlike that of the contemporary student who marries to satisfy social conventions and parental pressures, or that of the woman or man who marries again because she can't possibly raise a family on her salary or because he can't afford to pay a housekeeper and a baby sitter. Society has controlled sexuality by means that are much more subtle than laws. Most often it has been through a system of economic or emotional rewards and penalites.

Sociological studies have shown that sexuality is not only a personal phenomenon shaped by events and decisions of personal history; it is also a social phenomenon formed by the requirements and interests of the social organization. Gregory Baum suggests that the "puritanism" of the Victorian age was closely linked to industrialization and the expanding capitalism of that period. It was a time of hard work, dedication, and sacrifice of pleasure on the part of workers and even owners. In an age wholly geared to production, the economic organization needed a public morality that would encourage people to avoid pleasure, leisure, and experimental sexuality. No such rigidity in sexual life and ideals is evident in nonindustrial or preindustrial societies. Even medieval Europe made room for play and pleasure. However, in today's totalitarian states, whose main problem is still the production of goods, sexual norms and public morals resemble those of our own Victorian age, now left far behind by the postindustrial West.

This political dimension of sex — as a part of how we relate to our own sexuality and of our vision of church and societal authority — is often overlooked. Actually, it is to the advantage of the authoritarian structures that it be so. There is considerable evidence that, while sexual ethics have often purported to be prescriptions for reaching a personal ideal of purity or love, they have, in fact, usually functioned to mold persons to institutional interests and ends.

The theological basis that Augustine formulated was an accommodation to a social order based upon the family unit at a time when maternal and infant mortality rates were so high that women had to be forced, whether by physical or cultural means, to have babies. The economy and political structure of the time was based on kinship: the household was the productive unit; public decisions were made in offices handed down within families; the agricultural economy demanded much labor but needed very little capital. The family was, in fact, perhaps the only reliable basis for social order in an age of civil upheaval, wars, natural disasters, and poor communication. (It has even been suggested that a basic search for an immutable social order underlay the philosophy of the Platonists and Stoics from which Augustine drew.)

William Everett, among others, has shown the political ramifications of the sexual ethic in medieval feudal society:

> As the church was increasingly drawn into the orbit of the princes, a sexual ethic had to be evolved to separate it from the family-based power of the princes.[1]

But how was the church's power to be separated from the hereditary powers of the princes? By a way of viewing and living one's sexual life that established it as a new and separate entity: an ethic of restraint was the answer and it became as important to the church's integrity in a family-centered social order "as the constitutional separation of church and state has become under nationalism." Celibacy, defined strictly as an unmarried state, was and is an institutional policy evolved for institutional purposes. The purpose was, at that time, a legitimate one: it enabled the church to carry out its mission as a critical and prophetic agent in human affairs. It distinguished the church from the system of family power that held sway over secular matters. But gradually it was embroidered with theological and spiritual language to show its superiority to other ways of life.

The historical Christian analysis of sexuality performed a

two-fold social function. On the one hand, it sought to secure and promote within secular society a rational and stable social order that included hereditary offices as well as a procreative, unified family. On the other hand, within the ecclesiastical community, it helped to secure a separate identity for the church and an independent structure for its authority. The church needed a critical distance from secular ways of life to assert its dominion in the political order: this distancing fostered the idea of the primacy of the spiritual over the temporal—an extremely important chapter in church history, but one rarely analyzed in terms of sexual customs and teaching.

Such a perception of the societal character of sexual control may be disconcerting to those who have assumed the traditional teaching to be the "truth" in the sense of absolute, unchanging divine revelation. But that uneasiness can be cured by looking more carefully into the human history of this truth. The same societal conditions produced the traditional teachings on masturbation and homosexuality: it would be difficult to understand the strict prohibition of masturbation without seeing that it, too, was serving a strictly institutional purpose. To avoid masturbating was a way of internalizing the demands of the familial order. To masturbate was to reject these demands. It was, in effect, "cultural treason." To do it was to choose the individual self and useless pleasure over the goals and purposes of building the human family. If it seems excessive to cite the political implications of such a private act, one should consider the importance placed upon it by feminists within the context of "ownership" of one's own body.

To make use of such a fund of sexual self-restraint, the church itself had to project itself as a family. To the extent that the church imposed itself on the consciousness of its members as a special kind of family, it could impose its authority and demands on them, and especially on its leadership class. The notion developed of an alternative "family," in which *sexual nonexpression* was the sign of membership. The connection between chastity and obedience was emphasized and was never far from the conscious awareness of the members.

In our own time, when family order is no longer the model of societal order or authority, it becomes very difficult to transfer this self-restraint to the demands of other institutions. In a situation where human rights replace father-rights and the value of the human community replaces that of the family, discussion about the morality of masturbation becomes irrelevant — except perhaps within the women's movement, where it often functions as a first statement of independence. (Opposition to self-pleasure, when it does occur nowadays, is often opposition to women's liberation rather than to the simple act itself.)

Similarly, it is impossible to understand the condemnation of homosexuality apart from the demands of the historically family-centered social system. From a family-centered point of view, homosexuality constitutes an attack on the procreative unit. Procreation was a duty in an economy based mainly upon labor. Nonprocreative partnerships also threatened institutions based upon heredity. Insofar as it provides an alternative model of intense personal relations, homosexuality was thought to undermine the "normal" patterns that were assumed to be "necessary" and "natural," but were, in fact, responses to social conditions.

From the point of view of the church, homosexuality had to be prohibited so that the hierarchy composed exclusively of men would not lose its rational ordering. An organization cannot work effectively if the relations among its officers are deeply affected by purely personal ties. A weaker form of tie, the "particular friendship," was also seen to be a threat to the effective working of the group, and it was rejected in groups of religious men and women in favor of a "universal charity" that was rational and controlled.

Theology invariably follows practice — but in all human affairs, practice flows from many factors, including ideology. As a social situation changed, the church's need to set up a separate "family" structure diminished and the practices of particular friendship and masturbation, among others, caused less institutional concern. Margaret Farley has observed that "the reason increasing numbers of theologians are no longer hostile to masturbation or homosexuality is that these proscriptions no longer have an adequate institutional basis. They no longer make social sense."[2] When they did make sense, they made social sense, and must be judged within their social context: access to social power was once obtained through family; now it is obtained through money, gender, or knowledge.

Those who argued for the superiority of celibacy claimed that it made the search for perfection easier and service more single-minded by doing away with the burden and distraction of a (competing) family. In this privileged state the priest was taught that he could pursue his vocation without being dragged down by secular and material concerns, and could tend to his spiritual development without the disturbing effects of physical pleasure.

The masking, whether deliberately or not, of the political reasons for these sexual restraints took two forms. On the personal side, it took the form of a biological naturalism wherein social interests were overlooked and the natural requirements of the male organ itself were absolutized. On the ecclesiastical side, it took the form of a spirituality wherein the total human being was overlooked and the nonbodily aspects of life were absolutized. In both cases the institutional concerns were lost from view: the purely occasional rationalizing of sexual control became doctrine and the changing social context, with its demand for flexibility, was overlooked.

The church's amnesia about the origins of traditional concepts may have been fortunate, if not blissful, in its time. The distance the church achieved from the competing institutions of the patriarchs and princes—along with its ability to criticize them, coerce them, and at times cajole them—would not have lasted long if the church had openly announced that celibacy was one of its main safeguards against their quest for total power. Nor would it do to announce that masturbation and homosexuality threatened the family structure, while prostitution and rape did not. Unfortunately that amnesia now blocks our present social task, which is to develop a new understanding of sex that takes today's institutions and social purposes as seriously as the old understanding took the circumstances of its era. And though it will be shaped by global, economic, and organizational concerns, just as the previous one was, our new sexual understanding must be carefully constructed so as to serve human equality, dignity, and growth, and not only social needs.

In chapter 7 I will attempt to indicate in broad strokes the lines along which such an ethic might develop. There is another priority, however, and that is to try to show with more depth the meaning of human sexuality in the late-twentieth-century Western world. Our standards of behavior exist, after all, to protect values; and values are meanings "perceived by the heart" as essential to living our lives as human beings.

Neither the need of the race to survive nor the interests of the social system within which human beings must live sufficiently explain why sexuality belongs under the heading of "social justice." The concept of "relationality" does explain why.

Prior to the question of functions is the question of meaning. The inner meaning of those acts by which men and women express their love and desire is that of communication. The person is directed outward, toward others. What we call our sexuality is that bodily capacity to express our need for others and seek fulfillment in sharing our own life and expanding it beyond the circles of body-self and family of origin. In fact, we might define the body as the system by which we call and respond to others. The ultimate effect is to create relationships and even, seen in the largest context, to produce one's world. When human sexuality is discussed, it ought to be discussed under the rubric "The Relational System." The desire is for union, even though one effect may be procreation.

The unity of the world may seem a far-fetched and difficult notion to accept as the meaning of human sex. After all, phrases like "a fire in the loins" or "a gleam in the eye" have been used to describe the urgency of sexual attraction and pursuit. Though colorful, such phrases are reductionistic. They tend to reduce the whole process to a biological goal with a "before" and "after." Those phrases worked well to characterize sex as the drive to set up a new family, when that was the overwhelming need. Moreover, the need served by the family was more one of propagation than one of companionship. All this was neatly expressed in the use of the tag "reproductive system" for the whole of human sexuality. But every time a social change produces the need for different behavior, there develops a corresponding need to think about and talk about things in a new way. Only then can we "know" what we're doing. Animals, for all we can tell, have no such need. But for human beings, for whom the brain functions as the primary sex organ, the new aspects of their lives need to be illuminated with new words and phrases.

This reformulation must be done regularly, but not necessarily continuously. It must be done when people become aware of something as problematic, when it doesn't seem to work as smoothly as before. Lewis Thomas speaks of a human need to philosophize that is as essential for functioning in a cultural and social milieu as food and drink and exercise are for keeping physically fit. He calls it primitive humanity's penchant for "transcendental metaworry": In a humorous bit of fantasy, he imagines prehistoric man discovering his thumbs, "staring at his hands, opposing thumbtips to each fingertip in amazement, thinking, by God, that's something to set us apart from the animals — and the grinding thought, What on earth are they for? There must have been many long, sleepless nights, his mind all thumbs."[3] Thomas continues with images of ancient fireside committees, convened to argue whether this thumb thing wasn't going too far and that perhaps we'd be better off not using them at all. Actually, none of the wise answers to the question "What on earth are they *for?*" has been adequate for all time.

The power of our sexuality has frightened more than a few into joining the subcommittee that argues "better not touch." It has set many others to reflection, at various levels of sophistication. Not much theology and philosophy has dealt with it (these graze in the nearby and safer fields of marriage and love, and occasionally throw a glance or take a potshot over the fence); some technical analysis and how-to literature has been written, and a vast bulk of oblique but worried rumination has grown in the form of jokes, popular songs, television shows, and pulp-magazine stories. All of it demonstrates the need to continue to explore the question "What on earth is it *for?*"

The answers, tentative and inadequate though they appear to be to each succeeding generation, show at least two things: how essential for and even constitutive of human life this impulse to relationship is and how historical, or changing, this reality is. It was once thought that the search for the unchanging "nature" of human things would yield an unchanging and permanent core from which unchanging and absolute rules of use and behavior might be devised. But not only must the answers change—even the question is changing. "What is *it* for?" becomes "What are *we* about?"

We are recognizing that sexuality is not a gift we possess in a static mode, but a dynamic *we are*. Any statement about sexuality is in relation to us and our changing situation. Neither term can be fixed without the other. And increasingly we know that most meanings of things, including thumbs, are multiple, and the "what" in "What is it for" is an elastic word that stretches with human experience, both individual and communal.

One could formulate a kind of "law" of meaning as follows: the most reliable interpretation is the one that embraces, but goes beyond, past formulations. The insights of the past into sexuality as biological and personal are not negated but included in this present understanding of it as relational and social—as the relational system whose purpose is unity. The compelling model of our human sexuality is mediation, that is, bringing persons into relation, rather than simply creation, that is, bringing babies into being. Gabriel Marcel, trying to make the point that procreation is more than biology, has written that human creation is more accurately seen as mediation, the function of midwife rather than of originator, and the appropriate image is mother rather than father.

All of this is to indicate that sex, like love, has a development and a history of its own. The complexity of present-day experience involves new factors that need to be taken into account as we form a Christian theology of sex: we require a *reconception of the meaning of sex*, starting from what "is" rather than what "ought" to be; a *discovery* (not invention) *of new forms of expression*; and a *transformation of those images of love and sex* that have been stereotyped and made impotent.

The factors that contribute to the new setting within which human love operates comprise a list as long as a therapist's arm, and they have been formulated in as many ways as there are authors who have attempted their analysis. Among these factors are the psychological self, the anxious self, the power of modern technology, and the new and unprecedented demands of the "world community."

First, the psychological self, with its self-affirming drives (evident in the somewhat narcissistic human-potential movements of the 1970's) and its self-escaping drives (evident in the drug and pop-music cultures and religious cults among the young) must be held together in today's precarious freedom of role changes and identity problems. Those who work with unwed mothers and promiscuous teenagers report that a negative self-image is usually at the root of their problems, and when an intensive program is undertaken to improve their self-image and sense of self-worth, their sexual problems are resolved as well. The attempt to deal directly with the topic of sexual behavior — whether through moralizing, law, or education — fails, perhaps because sexuality is an expression of the difficulty rather than a cause of it (in much the same way as our society fails when it addresses itself to the effects rather than to the causes of poverty).

Second, the anxious self, which experiences its finitude and limitation, must learn to live with hope on the boundary between life and death, being and nonbeing. Anxiety in the sense of existential angst is a modern phenomenon. The attention of the self has turned inward in response both to the discoveries of psychology during the last century and to the decrease in the amount of time required for meeting the physical needs of food and shelter and the often overly rosy view provided by television of how other (mostly fictional) people live and feel and communicate. The secularization of modern life has unwittingly added to this anxiety by suppressing the rituals by which the person once got into connection with other human beings past and future and with a loving center of the universe.

In an age of anxiety and alienation, such forms of exploitation as pornography, wife beating (with accompanying husband killing), and child abuse are found to increase. It is not surprising that the most intimate relationships register with great sensitivity the increased stress of modern life. What might be surprising to some is the suggestion that this distorted sexual expression is not the result of a loss of morality or of freer sexual standards, but is the early-warning system of another deep-seated social problem. History shows that periods of excessive emphasis on sex very often coincide with periods, not of affluence, as is sometimes argued, but of widespread loss of meaning.[4] It was in the "golden ages" of many cultures—imperial Rome, Tang China, Louis XIV's France—that sex became a preoccupation precisely when there appeared to be no more worlds to conquer. Moral depravity and corruption are often defined as increased sexual activity and are blamed for social breakdown, but the problem might more accurately be located as one of *occupational* imbalance. When the work to be done by a people or class or nation is not significant or sufficient, then distortions of sex seem to appear. In our day, the situation becomes self-perpetuating because, for the first time in history, we live in an era of mass communications.

New technological power, with its possibilities and threats, redefines our existence as persons in relationship to each other, to nature, and to God. Nature is now seen not as a nurturing mother or a source of "law" and patterns of conduct. Instead, it is viewed as a reservoir of power that can be manipulated as a means to an end. Nor is this the kind of power that contains limits to determine how it can be used. Nature's power is capable of being bent to the almost unlimited purposes of human imagination.

Our relationship to nature, then—even what might have been called "sexual nature"—has been turned upside down by technology. We no longer attempt to seek our destiny in faithful service to nature, but we force nature into service, through reason and skill, to realize our own purposes. This "desacralization" of nature is not necessarily worse than the preceding situation, but it is certainly different and more complex.

One of the effects of technological development has been the mobile society, with neither roots in the land nor a deep sense of roles and duties that a stable life provides. In what has been called this "throwaway" age, relationships are conceived of in terms of power and security. Relationships between men and women are revealing themselves to be attempts to impose power, power to attract or dominate, and to gain security in the form of freedom from loneliness and financial worry. The mode by which we live in a society is always characterized by a kind of pervasive unity; our view of nature as a usuable power affects our sexuality. This is another way of saying what was said in chapter 1—that we live "within" the myth, and from its vantage point we understand everything else. The myth of sex is that dominance and submission patterns produce order and security.

However, it is neither possible nor desirable for individuals who live their lives within the technological mode to try to isolate their sexual relationships within the older model of submission to "nature." The simple fact is that our world is being continually restructured through technology. Social analysts have identified the shift from an industrial society to an information society as one of the most powerful trends in the industrialized world. They predict that the impact of this shift will be more profound than the shift from the agricultural to the industrial society that took place in the nineteenth century. And almost everyone is aware of the effects on family life, choice of sexual partners, education, population growth, and lifestyle that were produced by industrialization. One might argue that the so-called "new morality" of the sexual revolution of the 1960's was only a late accommodation to changes that had already taken place but were not generally applied to women, who had not fully participated in the Industrial Revolution or were runaways from it, as the women of the 1940's and 50's who set up their households in the suburbs might be said to have been.

If postindustrial society is an information society, what does this mean for us? One of the first things to notice is that the typical American occupation is no longer farmer, as it was in the eighteenth century, or laborer, as in the nineteenth century, but desk worker. In 1950 the number of people in the information sector of the society was seventeen percent; it now exceeds fifty-five percent. Occupations within the information sector include positions in banks, stock exchanges, insurance companies, education, and government. In this information society the stategic resources are knowledge and data (by contrast with the industrial society with its strategic resource of capital). Knowledge is not only renewable, but it is self-generating; moreover, because it is in our heads, access to the system is much easier. This society holds a possibility of opportunity far beyond those in which one had to be a wealthy land owner or financier to gain access to the political and financial power of the system. It means that in knowledge is power.

Another trend that has been observed to accompany technological sophistication is that toward greater attention to human response. Here is the point where a recovery of a positive attitude toward sexuality becomes crucial. With the introduction of each new technology a "high touch" component has had to be built in for the technology to be accepted. With television came the "humanizing" response of the group-therapy movement that led to the personal-growth and human-potential movements; with medical advances came new interest in the family doctor, neighborhood clinics, the quality of death, and holistic medicine. It ought not to be surprising, then, that with the widespread use of the computer comes a revival of charismatic religion. The affective gains new value and power. All this has something to say to our understanding of the body, sex, love, and intimate personal relationships. In an age in which "skin hunger" has become famine, it is likely that dating and marriage will be used for satisfying the simple need for closeness, and such purposes are far more profound and less free than those presupposed by the traditional standards still accepted for matrimony. Perhaps it will be recognized that there have to be varying degrees of formal commitment, all sanctioned by society and blessed by a church, to correspond to the varying degrees of commitment and freedom present in individuals and couples. A series of "minor orders" leading up to sacramental marriage is not unthinkable, and, in fact, has been in effect in some societies. When there are not many brothers and sisters and not much social permission to cuddle and touch, marriages are likely to be entered into under false pretenses. The point here is that a "high tech" society ignores its requirement for "high touch" intimacy only at its own peril.

Our world community, the so-called "global village," demands practical action from us to meet its problems. Marshall McLuhan captured the new sense of interdependence among humans and nations when he said, "there are no passengers on spaceship earth. We are all crew." Probably the newest sense of being "crew" rather than cargo is that enjoyed by some third-world people, by some blacks and other minorities in the United States, and by some women.

Because of instantaneously shared information, we are now

potentially one world, and are in the process of sorting out very important issues. We have a sense that if we are to survive, we must learn to love, but it is not always clear what we must *do* when we love. Do we give food to the poor? Establish an agency? Have children? Work for zero population growth? Among issues requiring action and, therefore, decisions are the population explosion, poverty, the rise of new nations, and disarmament. When we become aware of these as *our* issues, the radius of our social responsibility is extended. Already the significance of public opinion for national policy in a country such as ours shows that just by *thinking* about a question we make some sort of response to it. But what has this state of the world to do with Christian sexuality?

The social realities of the twentieth century place demands upon Christian thinking about *all* important issues. This is a time when "dispossessed peoples" see hope for their participation in planning the use of the world's resources. As this struggle comes to be grasped in theological terms as "God's struggle" or as "God's will for us," it must be related to the Gospel message to share God's creation with all the people. This is translated into a religious commitment to the poor of the world. It is only within this context that the relationship of sexuality to religious belief can be discussed meaningfully.

It has become clear that a privatized religious sense, including the privatization of sexual morality, has effectively separated the ideal of being holy from the mandate to effect justice. In Protestant churches the concern has been for local fellowship and the individual conscience. The Catholic church has focused on a morality of obedience to established authority. Neither has been effective in protecting the disenfranchised and both have succeeded only in stifling meaning and relationships. The current trend of the world economy is to systematically deprive whole peoples of any possibility of deliberation or choice in their own regard. The expectation of survival for an elite one-third of humanity seems to require the nonsurvival of the other two-thirds and is fast becoming formal policy. The assumption behind it is the "filter down" theory, by which it is argued that if the property of the advantaged is protected, and if the elite are at the same time taught noblesse oblige by a supporting church, they will open their hands and hearts to the needy.

In traditionally male-oriented morality, a similar assumption is at work: "Women, obey your husbands; husbands, *love* your wives." The appeal is to the "higher virtues" of the men, but with little protection for women when such generous feelings are lacking. The appeal to women, however, is less an appeal than an ultimatum. Their freedom to consent is often an illusion; the reality is their need to be compliant in order to share the goods of the system. The lesson of history has been that when charity is preached more than justice, the outcome invariably serves the interests of the elite.

As long as the central human need was the production of children for survival of the human race, it was essential that religious symbols idealize the procreative endeavor above all other aspects of sexuality. Today, however, the size of the world's population, together with knowledge of artificial insemination, sperm banks, cloning, and in vitro fertilization, make an adequately peopled world practically certain. Now the more serious problems are *who* will live, and how; who will die; and who will make these decisions. No longer is it feared that the human race might die out; rather, the danger is that some people might face extermination or destruction for the sake of others' comfort. These people are the poor, the disenfranchised, and all who are vulnerable to exploitation.

But the structures for decision making in our world still affirm the tradition of father-rights. Those who wield the power fear the great numbers and the potential violence of the oppressed majority. This fear leads rulers to affirm even more strongly those things in the tradition that give legitimacy to their right to rule. Christians who understand the Gospel message as a mandate to serve God by serving the oppressed are caught in a double bind in which the choices seem equally dreadful: accept the situation of an established elite being served by the subjugated masses, or expect the total extinction that would result if the system were to fall to the "enemy."

Human beings — basically religious as they are (in the sense of needing to live within the sacred, or meaningful, as opposed to within the profane, or unreal) — deal with the dreadful by processes of symbolization and sacralization. In our world, it is clear that the patriarchal family is being desacralized as the model for businesses, industries, governments, educational systems, and other organizations, including churches. As people learn that the authorities who make decisions on their behalf often make them against their interests, the authorities lose their "sacred" status and their power to command a following. No longer is a "pretend" family, with its authoritarian structure, desired by students, workers, or churchgoers. An American example of the desacralization of authority is the trend toward decentralization in the political process, as well as in business and industry: the power continues to shift from federal to state governments. In state governments, there are more referenda, so that many more issues are submitted for popular vote.

What desacralizes a symbol is its loss of meaning, usually a practical and very nonmystical process. An instrument of our technological age can be given some of the credit for liberating people from the need for patriarchal authority. In the past, at least in business and industry, and probably in religion, it was necessary to have a hierarchy in order to keep track of everybody. Now, with the computer to keep track, there can be a restructuring into horizontal organizations composed of many small and enterprising groups. The pyramid has been outdated by the new technology; the patriarchal church has been called into question by the household church.

Whether through disillusionment or through the power of a new and better model, the patriarchal symbol has become ineffective in our day. It has lost its power to persuade. Self-representation and active participation are the watchwords of developing peoples and individuals. Today, "father-right" has been replaced by human rights as the ethical norm for international as well as community relations under the law. The sacredness and naturalness of hierarchy and bureaucracy, once affirmed by both religion and science, are called into question because of the exploitive uses to which they have been bent.

This affirmation of human rights must be recognized as affecting sexual relations as well as racial and international relations. It provides a context for the emergence of new relations between men and women that do not rest primarily on biological differences associated with the bearing of children. Just as it has become possible to see the world as it appears in the experience of the poor, it has become possible to see sexuality as it is experienced by women. This new vision has transformed consciousness, and it carries with it a responsibility. it is particularly appropriate that the response is a religious one with echoes in Scripture.

One of the functions of a faith community is to transform consciousness by giving new meaning to human action and assigning new value to human relationships. In the arena of sexual relationships, on a personal as well as on a global scale, we hope for a new sense of partnership, one in which power is balanced equitably and love is the love possible only between equals: free, mutually consenting and initiating, open to growth and development. The "charity" that characterizes a dominant-submissive relationship is being seen for what it is: a mode protective of an outdated cultural value. The Christian virtue of sexual love, on the contrary, is recognized as *reciprocally* self-emptying and *mutually* empowering.

5·

Monday: Buying the Field
*Sex as Personal Awakening
and Empowerment*

Sexual liberation would be far less important than we know it to be if it were simply a matter of fairness between two persons. In fact, it is much more than just another application of the principle of human rights. Fairness is administered under the law, that is, abstractly and without regard to personal uniqueness. What has come to be called sexual liberation, or the "sexual revolution," has been interpreted mistakenly as a call by women to have the same freedoms and rights that men have. But for persons, justice does not demand fairness, but *love*. If women are handcuffed physically with regard to their maturing as sexual persons, men are handcuffed emotionally. To have access to the same disabilities and immaturities as the other, the same promiscuity and alienation, is not liberation. Liberation, in sex as in every other area of life, moves one toward adulthood, responsibility, and participation in one's own and in others' growth to more complete humanity.

What makes this issue important for theology is an experience that is reflected in literature and poetry, as well as in the everyday lives of thoughtful individuals: the experience of a link between sexual awakening and personal awakening. To the extent that a person is deprived of the understanding and skills

needed for sexual development, that person is stunted in interpersonal relationships and in spiritual growth. One of the trag-
edies of the desacralization of sex in the Judeo-Christian tradition has been the impoverishment of the spiritual life of the laity,
among whom little or no understanding is cultivated about the
connection between the great part of their lives as women and
men, wives and husbands, lovers and parents, and the life of
union with God to which the Scriptures, their baptism, and
their preachers continually claim they have been called. With
the contemporary insight that human growth is growth toward
wholeness, we can overcome the dualism of the past and its rejection of the body and of the sexuality it falsely took to be identified with the body. A second insight is equally significant: spirituality, or growth toward God, does not require the rejection of
the human, with its intimacy, ecstasy, companionship, and passion; in fact, spirituality is Christian only to the extent that it
embraces and accepts the human. As John Dunne notes,

> As long as sexuality is numinous; as long as it is dreadful and fas-
> cinating, it is not yet fully human. The same is true of death. . . .
> Some kind of odyssey thus is necessary in which one goes from
> divine to human sexuality and from the power of death to the
> mortality of man. Somehow God must become man, the holy
> must become human. First there is an encounter with love, love
> in the form of numinous sexuality. Then there is an encounter
> with death, death in the form of a numinous power threatening
> one from the outside. Then there is a realization that one is mor-
> tal and a sensing of the link between one's mortality and one's
> sexuality. At this point one becomes fully conscious of being hu-
> man and is ready at last for a second encounter with love, for the
> consent to one's humanity which is the YES of love.[1]

Consent to one's humanity is not a small matter. Refusal of
one's humanity is, in fact, what the greatest theologians have
defined as concupiscence. As Schillebeeckx has pointed out,
Christians need to rethink the meaning of the human. The rift

between God and the human would vanish if we knew how to see the human, because, since Christ, what keeps God and the human apart is not a difference of substance, but a split in the mind. When a truly incarnational spirituality is accepted, the consequences for growth, satisfaction, and holiness in individual lives are revolutionary.

But the sacramental quality of human sexuality depends upon its personal quality. A love relationship can only reveal the quality of God's love to the extent that it *succeeds*, that is, to the extent that the persons know through it some of the many fruits of love. The task of this chapter is to suggest that the significance of sexual development shines even more brightly in the personal sphere than in the biological sphere. Growth to sexual maturity has more to do with becoming a person than with becoming a parent.

How, then, is sexuality related to personal awakening and empowerment? I began this book with reference to religious cultures for whom sexual intercourse was clearly a sacred act. It was designated as sacred precisely because it was experienced as power — power associated with the divine — delivered into the hands and lives of human beings. This was experienced not only as the uncontrollable and transitory ecstasy of the act, not only as the occasion of a new human life, not only as the bonding between individuals and the creation of social networks, but it was also experienced as effective in the cosmos, that is, as a cause of the crops growing, the animals multiplying, the rains coming. Whatever modern persons may think of this causal connection, the *conceptual* connection is crucial: sex, in its earliest understandings, is power. That power is divine, making for union with God as creator and lover. It is cosmic, making for order and creativity in the universe. It is social, making families and nations. It is personal, making — through rituals of initiation — the individual child into a responsible adult member of the community, empowered in relation to the self, to the society, to the cosmos, and to God.

With the reduction of sex to intercourse and intercourse to its biological issue came not only an overemphasis on the pro-creative aspects, but, more importantly, a loss of the sense of its relationship to the empowerment of the individual in growth to personal and social maturity. A disturbing example of this re-ductionism is the widespread tendency to consider the onset of menstruation only in terms of the young girl's ability to "get pregnant" and not at all in terms of her reaching a stage of per-sonal power and creativity. It is certainly possible to procreate without sex education, but without "intimacy-education" it may not be possible to reach true sexual maturity—or global human development. Some sense of the sexual dynamic involved in becoming a loving and responsible person is necessary to any expression of sex deserving the name "human." Sexuality is closely linked to the psychological development of the person and, through this development, to the human person's life of love in the world. The hunger for connectedness is not, in the final analysis, a hunger for physical relation alone.

"With sexual awakening comes personal awakening"—this is true even in our first experiences of the power of romantic love. Testimonies abound in literature, music, biography: a "new life" begins and is sensed when one becomes aware of the power of an-other to stir feelings and desires in oneself. Growth in self-con-sciousness as a person is the object of the human search for mean-ing. And growth in self-consciousness occurs when one awakens to the fact that one is drawn irresistibly to some form of presence and union with another. The orientation toward another that is the fact of our sexuality can be the deepest, the most unexpected, and the most promising experience of our own selfhood. More-over, self-knowledge is gained on a new level with each deeper level of knowing another. I can know myself completely as a sex-ual being, that is, as a female, only with the knowledge of another as male. And that is to know myself more completely as a whole person, not essentially as half of a couple. It is not he that com-pletes me, but, in relation to him, *I am* more complete.

Being and becoming involves the personal—hence, sexual acts of knowing and loving—but it also involves freedom, and as one matures, the development of more profound levels of freedom. The most basic freedom one has is the freedom to give or refuse one's presence to another. (This is just one of the reasons why rape is so reprehensible. Self-possession exists in direct proportion to the freedom one has to bestow or refuse one's presence.)

For the individual, life can be seen as a passage through various stages, each of which presents us with specific tasks. Among these stages are those in which we learn how to get along in the world, how to love as a man or as a woman, and how to die as a human being. How we approach work, sex, and death determines to a great extent the success or failure of our lives as human beings. A child fears and desires the unknown, the world of adult work; a youth fears and desires love; and an elderly person fears and desires death. To learn to love is both the delight and the duty of the sexual being, that is, the human being.

There is another aspect of the growth of personal consciousness that appears to be related to the growth of sexual consciousness. This is the development of a sense of time. Seizing time is tantamount to freeing oneself from imprisonment in the everyday, the routine, what the Greeks called *chronos*. One is opened to a large sense of time, to *kairos*, and thus to the reality of the sacred. Both in the individual life and in the history of the human race, the awakening to a sense of history, the development of a sense of the larger meaning of time, seems to occur as sexuality and mortality come into consciousness.

The awareness of sexuality thrusts a person into a dilemma precisely because of the intensity with which one begins to sense one's connectedness to others and to the world. Not only is one caught up in an attraction that makes the other vital to one's happiness, but one is also made aware that childhood's notions of autonomy are no longer supportable. The experience is that of being grasped by a power greater than oneself—however much this is ridiculed by cynics, it remains the experience of adult sexuality. One is taken up in spite of oneself, taken into a cosmic exchange whereby life is given and received and in which the power and the fulfillment derived from that power are greater than the individuals involved. A moment of encounter (*chronos*) becomes a moment of recognition (*kairos*), and all one's past and future stand in relation to this event (as surely as the hills surround the jar in Tennessee).

The experience of sexuality helps people to come to terms with their mortality. Women's experience of letting go, of not attempting to control what comes to them as an aspect of reality beyond their will (such as the experiences of menstruation and pregnancy), are said to prepare them for the total acquiescence that is death in a way that male sexuality, interpreted largely in terms of individual performance and conquest, cannot match. In other ways, too, sexuality and mortality are linked: through intimations of mortality, human beings are driven to create with urgency and passion. Moreover, for the discerning, sexuality carries clues to an existence in loving union beyond what we experience on this side of eternity. What it evokes in us, human love and desire cannot fulfill. It requires God for its completion.

The pleasurable and playful aspects of sex make it a profound source of personal power for the human being—power in the sense of effective and satisfying expression of what it is to be oneself, to be a free, knowing, loving being. The aspect of power that has been fearsome, and therefore rightly controlled in sexual relations, might be described as exploitation, manipulation, or the use of another by physical or emotional force as means to an end. Exploitive and experimental use of others for one's own physical gratification falls far short of the meaning of human sexual partnership. Exploitive sex victimizes and dehumanizes; loving, playful sex communicates knowledge and love of the self, of the other, and of God.

Sexual pleasure was rightly held in awe by the ancients because its intensity made it different, not in degree but in kind, from other pleasures. One might question whether the source of its intensity was divine, demonic, or chemical, but it is certain that sexual pleasure was *ecstatic*. The ancient insight that is important for men and women today is this: ecstatic experience — aesthetic, sexual, or mystical — restores unity to the chaotic and fragmented character of human existence. Ecstasy is not a luxury reserved to the human elite; it is a necessity for a restoration to wholeness of the experience of brokenness and dualism that are part of our contemporary life. Prayer, sexual union, and total response to beauty in music, art, and literature have much in common. They first point to, then induce, a healing sense of oneness within a world of tensions. And of these healing powers, the one found in sexual experience is the most widely available.

An individual's journey as a sexual being through the stages of a successful life should be characterized by an increase in the capacities for intimacy, self-expression, self-giving, and ecstasy. Limits are set, not to rob the person of self-knowledge, power, and pleasure, but to promote development for *all* persons in a world community.

One of the main contributions of modern psychology has been to confirm that mental illness, depression, and anxiety have their roots in the breakdown of human relationships. When relationships between people collapse or take hostile forms, people break down. After all, it is our relationships that constitute us as persons; and in all relationships we participate as bodily, sexual beings. Our basic need is to escape separations, to experience the satisfaction of determining, in part, the lives of others, and to be determined, in part, by others.

An individual cannot survive as a person if his or her experience is solely that of the repression of the emotions of the true self. Such an individual remains an uneducated child, untested, undeveloped. In effect, the *person* shrivels and dies from disuse. It is sometimes necessary to overcome fear and dread to be free to love, for Love is healing: one accepts one's finitude yet perceives the possibility of infinity. What is unnecessary and, therefore, wasteful is the fear and dread that have been arbitrarily associated with sex and have made sexuality another obstacle to self-awareness rather than a driving force of love. Sexual love, when it is mature, honest, and free, integrates and energizes persons.

It should be clear even from this brief treatment of the matter that both young people and the old have a right to their sexual development, a right not based on fairness, but on love for their unique capacities as persons. Adults who try to shield others from their own sexuality are cutting them off from the very realities of which they must have at least a vicarious experience if they are to become whole persons.

The deepest Christian insight into *human* being is that it is *ens amans* ("loving being"), that is, being which is unique by virtue of its power to love. According to Max Scheler, what separates humans from animals is neither reason nor spirit. These are different in degree but not in kind. What distinguishes human life is its capacity for self-transcending love between persons. Love, as the tendency of the individual spirit to go out of itself to participate in the life of the other, is the key to understanding and developing the human being, as well as to understanding the process of history. After all, the goal of history is *persons in love*, or, in other words, embodied spirits in communication with each other.

What needs to be done to achieve and increase personal and sexual maturity cannot be done by the individual alone. To assist the individual in negotiating the various stages of sexual and personal awareness, a series of ritual moments — celebrations — must be developed. This will not be easy in an antiritual society, but it is a method used effectively by religious groups. Ritualization becomes necessary when an action has lost its meaning or has been cheapened by lack of understanding. Ritual helps to name a reality as sacred, to move the individual from a known and safe stage to a new and sometimes risky future, and to connect the individual to all others, past and future, who have made the same emotional and spiritual journey. By heightening our awareness of the peak moments of personal development, such celebration would do a number of necessary things for us. It would link sexuality with religious experience, that is, with the sacred journey of the Christian through death to new life with Christ. And it would move the reluctant individual toward adulthood and responsibility for the quality of life and love in the world. It would also provide the comfort, support, and healing power of knowing oneself to be a part of a community with a common experience. Childhood self-discovery, lubrication and menstruation, erection and ejaculation, first intercourse, and all the stages of commitment and change, deserve to be celebrated in a human and a religious way. The personal power of an individual is measured largely by the degree of her acceptance and cultivation of all of her human potential — including her potential as a sexual being.

6·

Tuesday: Finding the Coin
Scripture and the Revaluing of Sex

No discussion of sexuality is complete unless it takes into account the Hebrew and Christian Scriptures. These writings have functioned for millions of human beings as source of revelation of God's initiative in relation to the human race and as reservoir of wisdom for how human beings should live in order to be worthy of that initiative. The Scriptures have also served, though less legitimately, as a sourcebook for judging others and making rules to cover every contemporary situation.

The Scriptures have much to say about the meaning and use of sexual power. Contemporary biblical scholarship has shown, however, that unless certain rules of interpretation are followed one is likely to come away from the reading of Scripture with ideas that are neither true nor useful. Historical scholarship has shown, not surprisingly, that scriptural sources have been cited in support of opinions or laws that have been formulated for political or social reasons far more often than they have been used as the basis of positions drawn primarily from biblical witness. Biblical commands and prohibitions have been employed with great selectivity by all Christian societies. What seems to be crucial is the *reason* for their use in each particular time and place. It should not be claimed that the theology is drawn from Scripture as water from a well — the relationship between the two has been more often one of coincidental similarity. We must remember that a theology that does not reflect the intent and broad themes of Scripture is not Christian; likewise, a group of ideas that merely reiterates empty formulas is not theology.

The Scriptures are not so much systematic books as they are a living tradition preserved in writing. They are much more varied and complex than is commonly supposed by those whose contact with the Bible has been in discrete dosages, like small pills premeasured to fit specific purposes. The Bible is neither a single book nor a single point of view nor a single authority; in its earliest form it was neither known nor disseminated as a unit. One would not have considered consulting it on urgent issues as an all-knowing authority. The "mirror, mirror, on the wall . . . tell me . . ." approach to Scripture is the product of centralization and polarization of authorities in later religious societies of the West.

Fourth-century Christian communities used the Bible as neither the only, nor even the principal, source of Christian ethical guidelines. Generally these communities conformed rigorously to the morals and customs of the cultures in which they were converted to Christ and where they learned to live as Christians. Basil, for example, used not only the Old and the New Testament, but found in classical literature — in the examples of Pericles, Euclid, Socrates, and other ancients — ethical models for Christian youth. Apparently he saw no essential difference between the ethical teachings of Plato and those of Paul. The early Christians seem not to have had a separate ethic.

Nonetheless, some radical departures from the values common in its time are reflected in the New Testament. Early Christians (sometimes) shared all their material goods; they (in some places) held an ideal of faithful lifelong marriage; and they (at one time) vowed in their baptismal formula that among them all oppressive boundaries of class, religion, and gender were overcome ("neither Jew nor Gentile, slave nor free, male nor female" [Gal. 3:28]). It has been said that the persecutions against the Christians were occasioned by their idea that the kingdom of God, whose arrival they announced, relativized all absolute claims of sex, marriage, and family, as well as those of society, culture, and religion. This eschatological overturning of values was as true for Paul as it was for Jesus: "When anyone is united to Christ, there is a new world; the old order has gone, and a new order has already begun" (2 Cor. 5:17). The Christian movement was characterized by a shocking (in its time) openness to all classes and races, to women as well as slaves and children. Such an inclusive message was bound to offend people who had seen another sort of righteousness as the condition for God's blessing. (Paradoxically, the eventual success of Christianity in the Hellenistic world can be attributed to the willingness of the majority of Christians to accept whatever the prevailing cultural tradition held to be true, honorable, just, pure, gracious, and good.)

Clearly, these Christians were not a people "of the book" in the sense of the Muslim's relationship to the Quran. They searched the Scriptures, but not for rules on how to live their daily lives. This "law mentality" was precisely what was repudiated, as the hypocrisy of the Pharisees, in favor of the freedom of the sons of God. However, they did look for models of faith and fidelity and wisdom: the earliest Christian teachings on sex and marriage drew support from the Wisdom literature, Proverbs and Ecclesiastes (common-sense material), rather than from Leviticus (law material).

One could, of course, treat the Scriptures *as if* they constituted an authoritative law book. One would then presumably look for the specific subject matter — sex, with all its subcategories and related issues — and attempt to construct, out of bits and pieces, a systematic treatment of it. However, the result would be a theology of sex constructed by only one person, with a limited point of view. Such a theology might help people to live their lives with satisfaction and free of guilt; however, it should not be passed off as "what Scripture tells us" or as "what God says." This has been done numerous times, producing various "moralities" of sex, each supported, in part, by Scripture. Some of these attempts occur within the Scriptures themselves, as when Paul works with some texts in Genesis to produce a partial theology of marriage.

From the outset, then, it should be recognized that there simply is no authoritative and systematic Scriptural treatment of human sexuality; rather, there are many possible theologies, more or less comprehensive, that can be produced in response to post-biblical concerns. One can hardly look to the Scriptures to identify a "right" or "wrong" view of sex. Nonetheless, one must respectfully compare one's best effort with scriptural sources to see if it coincides, in its central understanding of life and human destiny, with what earlier communities in similar situations have taken to be a faithful way of living and growing toward God.

The Hebrew Scriptures used sexual language and images frequently. The content of those passages, that is, what is intended to be communicated by them, is generally not something moral (about sexual behavior), but something religious (about the covenant). They used what they *knew*, namely, sexual experience, to try to understand the unimaginable — the covenant of God with the chosen people. We, by contrast, use covenant language to try to understand sexual relationships.

Another context in which sexual matters, especially detailed prohibitions, are discussed in the Hebrew Scriptures, is that of the social imperatives of the time. For the Hebrews, as for every society, sexuality is not just a leisure-time activity. It is rather a central pattern — like economics — according to which a society is structured.

The importance of procreation to the preservation of the people, especially after the exile, cannot be overemphasized. As has been shown elsewhere, the "blessing" taken by later interpreters to be a divine command (to "increase and multiply") occurs only in the priestly account of creation (Gen. 1), dated after 550 B.C., and not in the Yahwist account (Gen. 2:4ff.), which is dated earlier, around 950 B.C., before the need for a population increase was felt so urgently. In the earlier account, Yahweh's intent in creating male and female seems to be simply companionship. The experience of sexual being is cursed—that is, it becomes an experience of pain, manipulation, work, and domination—only as a result of faulty human choices. It is not portrayed as an intrinsic flaw in nature; nor is its negative form the will of Yahweh.

Even as Genesis affirms that all creation is good, it recounts the existential depths of destructiveness and exploitation to which the abuse of created realities like sex can fall. This has been read all too often as a description (or philosophy) of the nature of sex rather than as an interpretation of the unhappy experiences that are part of living humanly.

The Scriptures also serve to orient our faith and hope to a possible future. The whole truth about human sexuality is not fully communicated in the paradigm of the Fall, with its "submission and lording over" or its work and pain. Part of the truth lies also in the desire, fidelity, companionship, play, and ecstatic union of the sexual images in the Song of Songs, the Psalms, Ephesians, and Galatians, not to mention the joys and comforts of friendship and community reflected not entirely asexually in the Gospels.

The promise of sexual delight and mutuality, unkept in the chapters of Genesis, can be shown to be kept, after all, in the Song of Songs. Thematically and theologically, these two books of the Old Testament represent a unity: what need not be, but is because of sin (sexual patterns that are destructive), is shown in Genesis; what is not yet, but can be because of love (sexual patterns that are empowering and creative of love), is shown in the Song of Songs.

In a patriarchal society everything related to procreation is controlled by religiously legitimated rules. But the fact of such control cannot responsibly be used as evidence of any intrinsic defect in human bodiliness or danger to spirituality in sexual desire.

Other aspects of sexuality are also controlled because such control is viewed as necessary to the orderly continuation of a specific kind of social structure—male dominated and blood- or family-centered. The system itself is built on sexism, and therefore must control women's access to property, power, pleasure, and procreation. Matters like masturbation, homosexuality, rape, and prostitution are dealt with only insofar as they threaten inheritance of property and the purity of the family line. These matters were hardly even considered in terms of their threat to loving, faithful relationships between men and women. Once more, the form that this control takes is that of a system of external regulations and taboos enforced by ritual pollutions and purifications. Such a system of taboos must not be confused with moral absolutes. The Scriptures, both Hebrew and Christian, do give moral imperatives, but these are rarely commands detailing sexual behavior. In the New Testament, Paul distinguishes between taboo and morality. He uses different words for the two different concepts: one for sin or injustice in general (e.g., Rom. 2:12; 4:7; 2 Cor. 6:14; 2 Thess. 2:7; Heb. 1:9) and another in reference to idolatry, or violations of Jewish ritual purity in particular (e.g., Rom. 2:22; Tit. 1:16).

Because personal sexuality was not especially problematic for the Hebrew people, or because they dealt with it in other contexts — that is, as a matter of nature, not of sacred history, and therefore as a social, not a religious, matter — they simply did not regulate personal aspects of it. They were not concerned with sexuality for its own sake. Contrary to popular opinion, the Hebrew verb "to know" does not always have sexual connotations. It is rarely used in a sexual sense in the Bible (only ten out of the nine hundred forty-three occurrences of this verb in the Old Testament carry the sense of carnal knowledge).

One must remember that through the descralization of sex the Hebrews were able to distinguish themselves from the fertility religions of their neighbors. By assigning to Yahweh an asexual character the Hebrews distinguished their God of history from all the creator gods and goddesses of the surrounding cultures. Sociologically, it is a short step from distinct to superior, and where a specific sex act was prohibited by the chosen people it was usually because the act was associated with an alien culture and its worship of "false gods." Such acts were subsequently regarded as a betrayal of Yahweh through the practice of physical acts associated with a competing cult and culture.[1] This explains why certain sexual acts were deemed ritually impure, and why a taboo system evolved to protect the social body against pollution.

In every case, it appears that Old Testament legislation of sexual matters had as its motivation the control of procreation and inheritance or the control of alien religious practices and values. It had nothing whatsoever to do with the intrinsic value of one or another form of sexual expression. In the Hebrew Scriptures we see rules for ordering a patriarchal, and therefore sexist, society, as well as taboos for ensuring religious and ritual purity, that is, absolute protection for the status quo in the social structure and in religion. None of the specific laws of taboos should be seen to be immediately and infallibly applicable to a Christian society. As we have seen, Christian values specifically endorsed an inclusive community of faith—characterized by equality, mutuality, and freedom—under the single law of the love preached by Jesus. Christians' earliest interpretations of the significance of Jesus were based on the primacy of faith over law, on the total and complete rejection of taboos, and on the affirmation of prophetic freedom, of reason enlightened by the spirit, and of purity of the heart.

Nevertheless, the Scriptures are understood to be normative for Christians, for they do give infallible guidance. They tell the story of the covenant community in its response to God's initiative and they orient the Christian's vision of the new covenant community constituted by faith in Christ.

The New Testament is also far more varied and complex than is usually assumed. It is interested in the problems of power, justice, and the dignity of the dispossessed much more than it is in setting out a morality of sexual acts. In the New Testament's theology of the priority of persons over laws, of the weak and victimized over the powerful and self-righteous, and its message of the inclusion of all in the banquet that is the kingdom, we find its (largely overlooked) normative sexual morality. The New Testament references to prostitution, divorce, fornication, and "unnatural" goings on in no way rival in importance its concern for justice and love.

When the stories and sayings of Christ as remembered by the early Christians were first recorded, the fundamental assumption was that the church was the community of the last days. Jesus preached that the kingdom was at hand (Mark 1:15) and Paul's communities were convinced that "this world as we see it is passing away" (1 Cor. 7:31). Hence, it is not surprising that the New Testament is relatively silent on the everyday aspects of living one's sexual life. Jesus does seem to have some new teaching on the topic of marriage as it was "in the beginning" (i.e., before it became a field for exploitation?). He addresses a question more fundamental than that of lawfulness; he addresses himself to what *ought to be*, and in so doing he positions himself firmly against what was, in that society, a male-only right to initiate divorce. He insists upon the fidelity required in marriage as a sacred relationship, and he cites in support of his position Genesis 2:24, that is, the Yahwist writer, champion of mutuality, equality, and companionship-love (Matt. 19).

In general, Jesus moves away from taboos and the designation of specific acts as ritually polluting. He recognizes the orientation of the heart, and treats with care and dignity the marginal and "irregular" people of the society: adulteress, prostitute, leper, and tax collector. Moreover, Jesus is remembered by the early traditions as having moved away from rule making and law giving. When asked, "What should one do?," he tells a story. It is clear that his followers eventually got the point, for in their later efforts at producing guidelines for a Christian lifestyle, they felt free to innovate and to move away from the specifics of the old law and even from Jesus' own words. Paul, for example, does not claim that Jesus is the source of his teaching (1 Cor. 7:26f.), yet he teaches authoritatively.

Paul is also the theologian most responsible for clarifying why Christians were not bound by the dietary and ritual restrictions of Jewish law nor by its rule of circumcision. In some ways this is remarkable, for Paul's commitment to Jewish law had defined most of his life. It is also ironic, for Paul's writings are most often cited as *the* Christian way by those who wish to enforce a legalistic sexual ethic. Actually, eschatological expectation, social criticism, and moral guidance go together in the writings that have been ascribed to Paul. Christian behavior ought to be different from that of "ordinary men" (1 Cor. 3:30) — this means a different attitude toward women, who can be "fellow workers" (Rom. 16:3) and who as wives are to be loved (Col. 3:19).

It also means a different attitude toward work as a positive good rather than a necessary evil (2 Thess. 3:7-10). For Paul, Christian sexuality had little to do with "purity" ("all things are lawful to me" [1 Cor. 6:12]) or with procreation as justification for sexual pleasure ("to avoid fornication, let every man have his own wife" [1 Cor. 7:2]), but was rather a question of good stewardship. Sexuality, like other resources of the human being, was to be put to the service of God, not allowed to become obsessive and dehumanizing ("all things are lawful for me, but I will not be brought under the power of any" [1 Cor. 6:12]). Nor was anything to be done that would cause scandal or distracted one from the service of the Lord (1 Cor. 7:35). Virginity, as a witness in some parts of the church and at some periods, can be understood in these terms. When *all* use of sexuality is deemed to be dehumanizing, it makes great sense to forswear it entirely. It does not follow, however, that the use of sex is always dehumanizing or that the best way to reclaim it for God's service is to forswear its use.

To me the most significant statement in the New Testament is in Ephesians 5:22-33. This passage effectively overturns the naturalistic approach to sex of the Hebrew Scriptures and re-sacralizes it for Christians who intend to create loving and faithful sexual partnerships. This statement becomes a historical reality in the history of Christian practice when marriage is viewed as a grace-giving sacrament and celebrated as such. For persons of faith baptized into a new mode of life in Christ, sexual life is not left behind. It is a "great mystery," the making present in the love of a woman and a man of God's love for humankind.

Interestingly enough, this passage opens with the imperative "therefore be imitators of God" and closes with one of the ways in which this can be done: by the joining of two—the great mystery that reveals the revelation of God's love through Christ. The author is saying that as Christ is to God, so the one-flesh couple is to Christ. This is a priesthood of love. Christ is the place of, the revelation of, the *experience* of God; human beings united in body and spirit are the place of, the revelation of, the *experience* of Christ. It could hardly be clearer that the writer to the community of Ephesus is telling them that in Christ even sexuality is transformed and that sexual love is sacramental. Unfortunately, the point of this passage has been largely overlooked, even trivialized, because it has been used to enforce a culturally conditioned *rule* ("Wives, obey your husbands.") rather than to illustrate the theological *meaning* it contains. Sexual love is capable of being not only an experience of grace but also a revelation and a ministry to the Christian community.

With the re-sacralization of sexuality, the polarity of sacred and profane returned. When the Christian community slipped back into a negative view of sex following the dualistic philosophies of the surrounding culture, it slipped not simply into the naturalistic and socially cautious mode of the Hebrew Scriptures, but rather into a view that identified sex with sin and animal existence. The profaning of sex took place over the first thousand years or so of Christian theology. The third thousand years will, we hope, be devoted to the re-sacramentalizing of all human activity.

7·

Wednesday: Calling the Neighbors
Toward an Inclusive Christian Ethic

In dealing today with our own sexual lives and those of our children we find that we have lost a sense of the body and of sex as sacred and as capable of revealing God to us. What we have retained is the fear that the body is demonic and will overcome us if we relax the restraints we have so laboriously constructed and so strongly reinforced with arguments from the Bible and from traditional theological interpretations of the laws of nature. And even when we do accept modern medical and psychological findings about reproduction, sexual arousal, intercourse, and orgasm, we keep these separate from our discussions of social values and communicate them as knowledge of human "plumbing" relevant only to our biological functioning.

The human race is far from understanding its own sexuality in a wise and generous way. The task of reexamining our knowledge and ideas about our own sexual power is a never ending and increasingly worrisome task. The present moment in this process, however, is especially crucial because of the obvious failure of the Christian ethic to enable persons to live out the ideals of lifelong and creative fidelity and to prevent the violence, abuse, and exploitation of the weaker by the stronger in the name of sexual passion or right. And perhaps even more importantly, the present moment is crucial because of the new situation in which all human beings now live.

Our new situation has been defined as the stuggle for control over the resources of the world — the materials for feeding, clothing, curing, educating, and developing the four billion people who now inhabit the earth. Such a struggle must require all human beings to take a stand, to define the meanings and values at stake in this world situation, and to make choices for responsible action. It must require that Christians interpret the Gospel and its mandates in the light of a new awareness that our planet is strictly limited, and in the light of the fact that multitudes of human beings are newly striving for what they see to be rightfully theirs.

Nonetheless, to seek a simple panacea, such as better birth-control or population-control methods, would be to miss the point entirely. We must have the courage to respond to a newly conceived meaning of sexuality. As Karl Rahner has said, there comes a time when one has to stop sharpening the knives and *cut* something. But we must also be careful: a precipitate and simplistic jump from insight to law-making often reduces a multifaceted reality to only one of its dimensions. This is exactly what happened when the meaning of sexuality was reduced in past religious and family teaching to procreation, which is only one of its meanings. While it is true that focusing on that single aspect served the social needs of the time — that is, the needs to fill the known world with people and to "build the city" — it is also true that such a focus diminished the reality of sex in the understanding and experience of people, and robbed them of other authentic and useful aspects of the sexual experience.

What I intend to do in this chapter is, therefore, not merely to draw a different conclusion from the premise that sex exists for the purposes of procreation, but to shift the ground of the argument entirely. I have proposed a one-hundred-and-eighty-degree turn in religious thinking about sex, viewing its meanings as social and historical rather than as individualistic and biological. I believe that unless the question of human sexuality is seen as a question of social justice, it cannot be adequately formulated for our time.

To say that sex is a social-justice issue implies at least three things: First, that it is a social reality influenced by, and in relation to, other social factors of our time; second, that adequate sexual ethics will derive from the principle of justice rather than from an assumedly natural (biological) law *or* from a private search for self-fulfillment; and, third, that Christian social teaching provides an appropriate framework for responsible sexual decisions. I have argued the first point in chapter 4; now it is time to attempt to discuss the second and third points.

What sociology has made clear about sexuality is that the ethic which the church has continued to reinforce was the common ethic of Western society prior to the development of an enormous population base. The criterion for normal intercourse was that it inseminate the woman, for that was "what nature needs to get done." As we have seen, nature no longer needs as much fertilization, nor must fertilization occur in the same way. We can deny it, discuss it, and deplore it, but the education we have already given to our youth will enable them to discover the potential for planned populations, not just on the scale of individual family planning but on national and worldwide levels.

Catholic doctrine on divorce, birth control, and abortion is slowly moving in the same direction as that of other Christian bodies with less hierarchical structures and freer decision-making systems. All of these religious groups have responded slowly to the pressure of population growth. The time it takes to go from experience to articulation to deliberation and judgment is what determines the different pace. The Catholic church is strong in its theologizing and its process of articulating experience; the Protestant churches, however, provide more effectively for the elimination of obsolete forms. It has become a costly mistake for the churches to continue to reaffirm a sexual standard based on outdated ideas of social needs while overlooking present needs. Once human rights and human community have been affirmed as values, the consciousness among the poor of the world of their right to participate in decisions affecting them can no longer be ignored. These assumptions challenge all notions of inferiority in sexual relations as in class relations. Two-thirds of the world now knows it lives in substandard conditions. Half the population of the world is becoming aware that it had been regarded and had regarded itself in terms of its sexuality as the property of the other half.

Once women are recognized as persons fully capable of sexual feeling and not as property, they can no longer be used to satisfy urges as prostitutes, toys, cheerleaders, or wives in bondage. Nor can they be used to market products for consumption or become themselves merchandise as in the vast entertainment industry. The sexuality of some people is now used to transform others into spenders and swingers. It has been harnessed to our postindustrial economy to create, by its evocative power, an ever expanding market of consumers.

Once human rights are sacred, equality of opportunity must be available to be enjoyed by all, men and women, whites and nonwhites. And when women's human right to personal education and professional training is provided for in our schools, as it is now for some, it can no longer be claimed that their place is only in the home. When homemaking tasks are shared by men and women, interpersonal skills need no longer be divided into "headwork" and "handwork," that is, active leadership for men and helpful cooperation for women. Children will always need to be cared for and socialized, but the task can become one shared by equals; moreover, it can expand to include members of the community not in the immediate family. One of the great contributions of Christianity has in fact been to relate individuals to communities beyond the family.

Much that has been interpreted as "natural" is in fact shown to be cultural in origin and to have served the purposes of authoritarian groups or individuals. Sociology has gone far to reveal the conditioning that underlies human roles and practices. These may have been necessary for survival at one time, but later they became functionally autonomous. No longer necessary for survival, the conditioning usually serves the self-interest of those who hold power. This process is facilitated by the timidity with which subordinates call for explanations and justifications from their superiors. Studies indicate that males have been more susceptible than females to cultural conditioning, particularly in the area of sexuality.

Once women are able to see beyond the traditional definition of their role in sexual relations as passive and receptive, they will discover a potential for greater sexual expressiveness. The passive role was supposedly determined by anatomy, but in fact was reinforced by erotic literature frequently written by men. A study some years ago attempted to test bodily arousal of male and female college students to explicit sexual films. Sensors were attached to the volunteers, who were asked to indicate by pressing a button when they were aroused. An entirely unanticipated result from the test was the recognition that the women's biological state of arousal was often far advanced *before* they detected it and pressed the button, whereas many of the men indicated that they were aroused before there was physical evidence of excitement. Women may now learn to identify and take responsibility for sexual excitement as such, and perhaps also will be able to free themselves from their unwillingness to enjoy it. In either case, they will be less inhibited in their ability to feel and express sexual pleasure. It is also necessary that they find the freedom to consent to or to refuse a sexual encounter. Too often what passes as consent is simply compliance with what they have learned is inevitable.

One has to take the question of social conditioning a bit farther, especially as it affects the pleasure associated with sexual intercourse. Could it be that the taboo developed over the ages to concentrate male desire on the act of intercourse had as its goal the propagation of the race and was functionally necessary for its survival, whereas the present acceptance of and experimentation in sexual behavior takes the focus off intercourse and is a preparation for the newer tasks necessary for the preservation of the race? The first half of that question is often asked, that is, what part do guilt and prohibition have in the stimulation of desire? The second half appears less often, that is, what social good might be achieved by reducing guilt and individual preoccupation with sex? The answer has implications that are radical. The universal ideal would then be not only to live but *to develop humanly* and *to help open that option to all people.*

These observations about conditioning by language and taboo have many implications for the new interest of Christians in the development of *community*, in contrast with the older and more recent attempt to sacralize *family*. Our religious language is rooted in patriarchal family terms. The word "father" is used for heads of families, for priests, and for countries, and has been extended to cover the relationships of corporate managers to workers and of psychiatrists to patients. In every case exploitation has followed domination. A woman can be subject first to her father, then to her husband, and finally to her son, apparently without the situation seeming unjust to the men involved. When women come to consciousness of themselves as human beings, when they see clearly that "male" prerogatives are in fact rights belonging to all persons, when they recognize the assumptions about women from which men operate—all of this will result in an irreversible revolution in male-female relationships.

The question of sexuality in the church has been so concentrated on the so-called "family" issues of birth control, abortion, and divorce—along with the issues of masturbation, premarital sex, and celibacy—that most men are not yet aware of the much larger general problem of male-dominated theological language, liturgy, and forms of religious education that deny women a place to celebrate life in the church. Fortunately, women and sympathetic men theologians are now aware of this problem, and are searching the Scriptures and the tradition to ask questions about sexuality that go far beyond the issues of marital intercourse and unborn life to the issues of human development. The mandate for this basic research and recasting comes directly from the church through the words of Pope Paul VI: "It belongs to the laity, without waiting passively for orders and directives, to take the initiative freely and to infuse a Christian spirit into the mentality, customs, laws, and structures of the community in which they live." An ethic of restraint for women, couched in the language of a male-dominated double standard, bears no similarity to an authentic Christian teaching on sexuality.

The women of the churches are discovering their common oppression with the poor of the world. Human personalities, female as well as male, call for communal structures that provide for development of their active side as well as their receptive side, not just as couples, but as persons whole in themselves. Recognizing the Gospel promise of redemption as wholeness, men and women can do something effective about the contradictory and irrelevant proposals that the church still offers as ethical solutions to problems of life and marriage.

There is an absurd logic to the situation in which both abortion and conception control are condemned, especially when a double standard for boys and girls is maintained with apparent approval. In another contradictory position, a method of birth control by rhythm has been affirmed since 1936, although medical science still has not discovered how to predict the exact time of ovulation in the menstrual cycle, and there is some evidence of increased incidences of mongolism with less frequent intercourse. Nor do church officials generally make research funds available for the continuation of this and other much needed research. Natural family planning, though enthusiastically adopted by some, is not viable for the majority of sexual partnerships. One would think that an organization committed to preventing abortion would encourage research and education in acceptable methods of conception control. If serious about continence and abstinence as the only alternative, such an organization should seriously try to teach young men to delay their sexual activity until they can provide a hospitable environment for children. Clearly, in spite of the occasional sermon on self-control, this has never been attempted. Rather, the attempt is to lay upon young women the moral burden of restraining the man or, if restraint fails, of bearing the consequences herself. As long as such dubious measures are being affirmed as sexual ethics, modern knowledge about the requirements of population control goes unaccepted or actively opposed by religious organizations.

Many of the conflicts generated in Christian marriage are in large part conflicts between people trained to accept patriarchal dominance but who live in a society where communal participation is the preferred experience. Sexism creates problems in marriage that no prohibition of divorce will resolve and that even counseling cannot deal with adequately. The patriarchal model must be replaced, in marriage as in other aspects of life, with the experience of mutuality and equality among human persons. Then love, which is only possible between equals, becomes possible and real.

It must be recognized soon that the major problem of sexual ethics for consideration by the church is the human rights of women in the consciousness of the men who manage the affairs of the church. A discipleship of equals is no less called for than a marriage of equals. As Sister Marie Augusta Neal has said,

> Willingness of women to live in a male dominated society will decrease rapidly as the rights of paterfamilias decline and the implications of full human rights develop. Population size makes it no longer functional to continue subconsciously the social conditioning operative in art, education, and the mass media—which perpetuates father-rights long after we have rejected them intellectually and replaced them at the value level with human rights.[1]

Traditional Christian teaching on sexuality has attempted to locate the meaning of sex in a notion of "nature." As we have seen, the biological approach that derived its view from an analysis of the purposes of the body used incomplete data, that is, it used only the male genital organ and its function of insemination as the basis for the analysis.[2] It thus took a focus that, aside from being a partial (and therefore false) view of human sexuality, was also basically individualistic. It drew conclusions about how individual male persons would deal with their bodies and their private actions with regard to females. What it failed to do was name sexuality as a political reality, as an instument and expression of social ordering. The exclusively male orientation of traditional teaching makes this oversight understandable. If the male defined his (and by extension, all men's) sexual nature according to the activity of his genitals, then the female was necessarily cast in the role of passive recipient or object. The recognition that it takes two to *procreate*, is not in itself acknowledgment of the true sexual character of the act.

When the wife and the family produced from her are all seen as extensions of the man, as his dependents, only one subject or agent is acknowledged; all relationships between him and other "true agents" (that is, all other property holders, citizens, or males, depending on time and place) are regarded as social and public matters, and social standards are applied to order them. However, relations between him and his "helpmate" are thought to be determined by the "natural law" of sexual acts as revealed in the structure and function of his penis. It should be noted that, even in New Testament times, in matters affecting *another man's* wife, social standards were considered to have been violated. The Commandments state, "Thou shalt not commit adultery or covet thy neighbor's wife"; but in matters affecting an unattached woman or "prostitute," there were no fixed social standards — this was a "private" matter. To this day, the rules of fairness governing man's relationship with man do not apply in the family or the sphere of his "private" relations with wife and children. So wife beating and child abuse, while universally deplored, fall into the category of private matters that patriarchal society in effect chooses not to control.

It has been estimated that in America today one out of every two wives has been beaten at least once by her husband. In fact, some segments of American pop culture are propagating a kind of "chic" brutality in which sex is connected with violence against women, often as part of the promotion of commercial products. The themes of sexuality and power, dominance and submission, are displayed in pictures of tortured or beaten women, usually gazing adoringly, or at least with pleading eyes, at the dominant males. The attitude that woman is an object to be displayed for man's pleasure is what engenders most pornography. While the women's movement has recognized the power struggle between men and women and tries to equalize power, this approach frankly celebrates the imbalance of power. Women continue to be regarded as fair game by people who would be aghast at the hazing of blacks or Jews. But worst of all is the assumption that women actually enjoy being dominated and brutalized by men: this is the establishment of violence as the ultimate aphrodisiac.

I do not claim that church teaching intentionally supports such exploitation. I do see, however, the same assumptions behind the media's use of women's pain and behind the church's emphasis on the martyrs among women saints and its celebration among the living of only the virgins and the self-sacrificing "angel-mothers."

One might point, however, to the church's public opposition to abortion as proof that it does speak out against violence and treat sexuality as a social issue. But when attempts are made to control the sexuality of women while not addressing that of men, the result is sexism, not responsible social concern. Moreover, it should be remembered that when women crept off quietly to do the awkward and brutal thing they considered necessary, but neither challenged the legal structure nor demanded adequate medical care, few voices were raised in outrage or sorrow. The Christian position on this issue has been based on the premise that sex belongs to the sphere of individual morality and is governed by the standard of the proper, "natural," disposition of male seed. The ground of the argument has to shift to "murder" before there is basis for condemnation, for the Christian position on that and other social matters develops out of the premise of the dignity of the individual human person and the needs of the community. The standards that have governed such matters as murder have included a kind of "ethic of conflict," an affirmation of the cardinal virtues of prudence, justice, temperance, and fortitude, with the immediate recognition that these need to be applied in the situation. It is not just the intentionality or "nature" of society that determines what is good or bad, it is the motive (intentionality) of the individual, the circumstances of the act, and its consequences for others.

My purpose has been to contend that sexual questions, in fact, belong in the sphere of social morality. To say that is not to be overly judgmental on the tradition: it was not possible to see sexual questions as questions of human dignity before women were recognized to be persons in their own right. But once that recognition is gained, the radius of responsibility is extended. People, including theologians and church officials, cannot meet that responsibility simply by repeating what hasn't worked in the past.

The church's teaching must be evaluated in terms of its effect on the attitudes and awarenesses of people. A new way of experiencing reality gives rise to a suspicion about our customary theological formulas, which in turn leads to new ways of formulating the truth that has been lived, thus beginning the whole process anew. The mandate to carry out that process is given with a simplicity and clarity that belies its revolutionary character. I cite Paul VI once again:

> If the role of the hierarchy is to teach and to interpret authentically the norms of morality in this matter, it belongs to the laity,

without waiting passively for orders and directives, to take the initiative freely and to infuse a Christian spirit into the mentality, customs, laws, and structures of the community in which they live. Let each examine himself, to see what he has done up to now and what he ought to do. It is not enough to recall principles, state intentions, point to crying injustices, and utter prophetic denunciations, these words will lack real weight unless they are accompanied for each individual by a livelier awareness of personal responsibility and effective action.[3]

There will be very little for Christians to celebrate and much guilt to bear in their sexual lives and in those of their children if the new social reality that challenges the adequacy of present teaching pertaining to sex, marriage, and family is not taken into account. The alternative is painful and embarrassing rationalization, with the most significant persons excluded from the deliberation about their own lives and actions. We will examine six aspects of this new social reality.

First, women are demanding control over their own bodies, minds, and hearts.[4] They are playing a new role in contemporary secular society, one characterized by freedom, independence, and public participation. Men who had thought that they themselves had control over their persons and roles have also found that what they have is often the product of an overrationalized education and conditioning that falls far short of the goal of human development. Under obsolete regulations with regard to birth control, abortion, divorce, homosexuality, and sexual relations outside marriage, the lives of both men and women are not yet categorized in sacred language. They need a voice to speak for themselves, out of their own Christian understanding of life in their conditions. It is insulting and ineffective to have church leaders speaking for them as fathers speaking for children.

Second, the family can now be regarded as the basic unit of society only in a psychological sense. It is important in the lives of its individual members, but is no longer the uniquely power-ful social, political, and economic force that it once was. Since this is simply a fact, the church must question its overwhelming concern with the family and almost complete disregard for other systems in society. The official church seems to have accepted uncritically the assumption that the family is the strongest and most influential unit and devotes almost all of its pastoral ener-gies to it. Other forces and groups need the church as well, to be their celebrant as well as their conscience.

Third, the longer average life span of persons in contempo-rary society challenges the traditional teaching on sex and mar-riage. In 1900, the average life span in the United States was forty-seven; today it is seventy-three. By the year 2010, accord-ing to a prediction of American Family Physicians, it should ap-proximate eighty-two. Longer life will give rise to a whole new network of relationships that will not conform to the ideal of permanent and reproductive monogamy. "Until death do us part" makes permanence much longer when it comes at seventy-five rather than forty-five. The importance of children (who are with their parents for twenty years out of eighty) diminishes in the face of such a long life. A group of couples celebrating their fiftieth wedding anniversaries made this point quite directly: they didn't want to talk about their children ("they have their own lives") when reflecting on the meaning of their own life together. And the possibilities for divorce in a doubly long life span increase greatly.

Fourth, most human beings are involved in some form of sex-ual expression. If one proceeds empirically rather than concep-tually, one perceives that sexual expression is essential to, even constitutive of, human life and personality.[5] Some ascetic tra-ditions suggest that sexual desire is a passion of the immature person and one that human beings could very well do without, or at least refrain from acting upon. In an age where the socially accepted lifestyles were limited to marriage and vowed celibacy, it may have been possible to convince people that there were vast numbers of other people using no sexual outlet at all. Today, however, with long life and the wide range of acceptable life-styles it would be naive to pretend that sexual expression is legitimately sought only by the married. The technological character of our culture may itself account for the intense search for connection with other human beings that underlies our sexual variety. The social fact of almost universal involvement in some form of sexual outlet, even only masturbation, cannot be ignored. Nor can it be judged from the outset as moral corruption. It has to be accepted as a fact that experience gives us for further reflection. A Christian ethic that urges complete abstinence is as useless in such a real world as a dietary regimen that says stop eating.

Fifth, sex, marriage, and family, while closely interconnected in most human experience, are viewed in contemporary life as separable. Some medical factors, such as conception control and the increased average life span, and some cultural factors, such as the social and economic independence of women, have made this separation possible. Marriage is entered into for its own sake, often for companionship, and not necessarily to found a family. There seems to be no inevitable or necessary connection between sex, marriage, and family that transcends human and social concerns. Of course, the family is still unsurpassed as the best place to raise children, in terms of both their individual well-being and their socialization.

A tendency to separate sexual intercourse from marriage is also evident. While marriage remains the socially sanctioned framework for the sexual relationship, actual practice shows much more flexibility. Moreover, such relationships are not seen simply as "lawless" by their participants or by society. With or without the support of the churches, new norms are arising that would establish the circumstances in which such relationships can be validated.

Sixth, genetic research will no doubt continue to create new possibilities and new problems. Much of this research is too new and too specialized for people to feel the full force of the issues it raises. Such possibilities as gender determination, manipulation of fertility and heredity, and growth of a fetus outside the womb are all in various stages of exploration; and it is likely that the list will grow longer. In 1962, Arthur Clarke projected control of heredity by 2020, bioengineering by 2030, and artificial life by 2060, on the basis of the time elapsed in the past between scientific possibilities and their realization. Such issues call into profound question the adequacy of our concepts of "natural law" to guide our responsible use of sexuality.

These social realities must be taken into account, not only as we attempt to make ethical judgments, but also as we discover and celebrate new levels of meaning. The meaning of human sexuality is rooted in the whole Christian meaning of life and not simply in the facts of a given culture, and yet the particular cultural contexts of human life are not *extrinsic* to it. Our cultural context permeates our lives, inside and out, as the air we breathe creates, in part, our speech. It seems clear, then, that the context of human life has changed sufficiently to require a critical reexamination of past assumptions and attitudes — and, where necessary, a radical reconstruction — of our search for the will of God in sex, marriage, and family.

Christian moral teaching, to the extent that it recognizes the Gospel as a mandate to transform human society, must deal with the possibility that the world in which it lives exhibits values that are dehumanizing and contrary to human good. Therefore, the task of Christian teaching must be carried out on two fronts: theology must defend the right to personal growth and freedom of sexual expression within the bounds of reason and love against the legalistic morality of the past, but at the same time it must renounce the artificial hedonism characteristic of a consumerist society. Moved by personalistic thought and responding to "the signs of the times," contemporary Catholic theologians have come to a more trusting, more affirmative, and more joyous approach to sexuality. In this they have in large measure updated the teaching to meet the best tendencies of the society in general, and have abandoned the overly biological understanding of natural law, expanding it to mean, "according to the nature of the *person* and his acts." This has been liberating to many Christians who had tried in vain to live their lives as if the old assumptions were still valid. But this represents only a part, and not the most important part, of the task. It often remains an individualistic and privatized understanding — though a more tolerant one — of sex, and fails to do the prophetic task of going beyond what society has already recognized as of value.

A religious view of sexuality has to be more than healthy; it has to be grace-giving. We have yet to address the not overly free, but *false*, view of sexuality that our culture forces on us. The need for consumers and the use of sex to lure them to buy essentially useless products pushes people into a fragmented and unreflective search for pleasure, very often the soon-to-be-regretted pleasure of the moment. The ultimate effect is the trivialization of sex, so that the possibility of this cheapened symbol carrying religious experience is greatly and tragically diminished. Religion has failed to say, not that there is too much sex, but that there is not enough *good* sex, and it has failed to say why. When divine love and caring and human dignity are connected with sex, the real sexual revolution will take place. The church's teaching on sexual morality, if it is to do its task adequately on both fronts, ought to make people aware of the power society holds over them. It will not so much urge "conscientious objector" status on the Christian with regard to the battle between the sexes, but will urge participants to help make sex safe for love.

In each individual life, moral decisions must be made on grounds that include the motivation, the quality of the act itself, the personal and social consequences, and the circumstances. This complex act of decision cannot be waived simply by taking over a generalization or a guideline from someone else. Nonetheless, thinking about sexual issues under the rubric of justice rather than that of "natural law" enables us to consider the implications of our sexual acts in a more helpful way.

Eventually every rethinking of a theoretical question has to culminate in a practical reorienting of the issues. We will now look at nine representative sexual issues within the context of the rewon values of bodiliness, pleasure, and the development of persons.

First, within marriage, degrees of sexual relationship need to be recognized by society and blessed by the churches. It is clear from the arrangements that exist that the range of commitments couples understand themselves to be making is varied, both in duration and in intensity. The choice is not between legal marriage and abstinence, but among a multiplicity of forms of caring relationships as couples. It is desirable that church and society continue to define marriage in terms of its potential to be procreative, lifelong, and loving. However, it is also desirable to find acceptable forms which do not aspire to this ideal of sacramental marriage. A privatized morality might say that when the love has gone out of a marriage it ought to be dissolved. A morality of justice would contend that the depth of consent that established the relationship does not necessarily erode with the feeling, and therefore it should be possible for a couple to come together or stay together "for the sake of the children." Social justice could require fidelity to the consent once given. This, of course, assumes something that is not present in many situations: two mature persons whose consent was in fact free and profound, and who can remain with each other in courtesy and friendship rather than in destructive hostility. It also assumes a network of support for the couple choosing this lifestyle.

Sometimes, divorce resolves a seemingly unresolvable conflict and also prepares for a healing process. A second relationship may be able to restore the individuals to the possibility of love. But marriage is much more than social and religious permission for intercourse between consenting adults. It ought not to be entered into without complete awareness and readiness for permanence and parenting. It certainly ought not to be entered into because alternative forms for ritualizing relationships are not available. With the disappearance of our society's inordinate and obsessive fear of sex, and the overcoming of the social and economic inferiority of women, will come, we hope, the creativity to recognize, in law and blessing, the variety and multiplicity of significant human relationships.

Second, the issue of pre-, post-, and nonmarital intercourse is problematic even as we try to name it, for through these conventional terms sexuality is reduced to intercourse and intercourse is reduced to its function of fertilization of the female. A sexual morality that does not give in to the temptation of biologism would recognize that the morality of intercourse, once conception control is a given, cannot be judged solely in terms of marital status. Obviously, when a child is a possible result of intercourse, it is immoral not to provide, so far as possible, for a stable home with loving parents, or, in other words, only within marriage does it seem moral to conceive a child. However, in the present situation, with no legal and religious forms of committed relationship other than marriage, nonmarital intercourse depends for its morality on the relationship of the two individuals to each other and to their wider societies and on the degree to which their sexual intercourse represents an authentic expression of that relationship.

Third, there is a vast difference between the situation of mature adults seeking to express a clear and tested commitment and that of teenagers curious to experiment. Teenage intercourse is very likely to be exploitive. At this time in an individual's life, the capacities for relationships, intimacy, and sensuality need to be explored and cultivated. The unequal development of boys and girls toward their sexual peak, however, makes it likely that what is sought by girls is a romantic experience and personal intimacy while boys seek genital expression. This is related to our present forms of socialization, of course, but moral guidelines are made in terms of present conditions. In a society in which experiential knowledge of sexuality is lacking in any ritual form, it is understandable that young people will seek such knowledge through experimentation with each other. It should be made clear, however, that other forms of experimentation (which do not use another human being as a means toward one's own goals) are to be preferred. It would be more in line with the Christian values of freedom, control over one's own person, and justice to seek experiential knowledge of one's own body and one's sexual relatedness through self-pleasuring or through vicarious modes of sexual arousal, such as literature, films, and other arts.

Fourth, what has been negatively referred to as masturbation ("pollution by one's hand") appears to be a different reality in the experience of males and females. For women, the question of self-pleasuring has often become a question of power over one's own person. Knowledge of one's own body has become identified with the right to one's own development. Self-pleasuring can be for women a political issue (one is not owned by another) and a personal issue (pleasure and fantasy are among the goods of bodiliness). It is not unlikely that in our time self-pleasuring will help to correct and heal the low self-esteem and failure to take responsibility for the self that some see as the form of sin that women have inherited.

For men, both the inevitability of using self-pleasuring as an outlet and the sense of guilt that often accompanies the experience seem to point to the basic relationality of their sexuality. In the service of relationality, self-pleasuring can in fact promote growth. At the very least, it can represent respect for the right of the female *not* to be available and *not* to consent. It is possible that it could correct the unbalanced autonomy and tendency to domination to which male sinfulness is heir.

Fifth, the presence of persons with a same-sex orientation has been constant within both Christian and non-Christian societies. Homosexuality has become a political as well as a social reality in the recent past. Because same-sex relationships do not affect the social structure of the procreative family, it is not a moral issue in the same way that procreative heterosexual marriage is. The same criteria should be used to judge homosexual relationships that are used in evaluating nonmarital heterosexual relationships. The morality that governs friendships, alliances, and relationships between persons of any sort is applicable to sexual nonmarital relationships.

Sixth is the issue of prostitution. What is generally meant by the term prostitution is the selling of sexual favors. This term is heavily loaded with negative historical and religious associations. It must be said that the exchange of cash does not in itself necessarily debase a human activity. The debasing aspect of this exchange is the victimization that is characteristic of the practice. Prostitutes are often recruited when they are financially destitute and at a low level of self-esteem. Methods of recruiting and maintaining women and young men to be used sexually for the gain of others are apt to be manipulative and exploitive. Not the least among the deprivations suffered by the prostitute is the loss of the capacity to experience human sexuality as ecstatic. Given the economic realities and present circumstances that surround the practice of prostitution, it is difficult to see how it could promote individual or social justice. Intrinsically, however, apart from the conditions that force consent and erode self-respect, prostitution may be morally neutral.

Seventh, it should go without saying that, according to the meanings of human sexuality explored in this book, incest and other forms of sexual activity that involve one powerful and one powerless partner are exploitive. The use of others, even with their collusion, is always immoral when it is accompanied by force or fear or lack of knowledge of the alternatives.

Eighth is the issue often called "swinging." In *an eschatological sense*, playful, lighthearted sexual interaction might be viewed as an ideal. Brief encounters are not necessarily less satisfying or less humanizing than lasting relationships. However, in the present age of inequality, jealousy, pride, violence, conflicting expectations, and incomplete self-knowledge it is to be rejected as impractical and potentially destructive of personal growth.

Ninth, celibacy, or abstinence from genital activity, when freely chosen with knowledge and love can be a social as well as a personal good. As Daniel Berrigan has shown, it can be a choice that frees the individual "for revolution." The individual without a partner or family is not tied to the structures of society in quite the same way others are. In its first appearances, celibacy was viewed and punished as subversive. Recent historical studies have shown that the celibate communities of women in the early Christian period provided an alternative to the patriarchal marriage patterns of the time. Women were required by law to be married, which meant in effect that they were to be in a state of submission to men. When the option of virginity was provided and protected by the religious authority, it served to free those women at least to exercise their talents and ambitions in spheres otherwise closed to women. Celibacy freely chosen as an option and a charism can be a means to personal fulfillment, a source of social reform, and the occasion of outstanding service to others.

There is also the possibility that those uncommon individuals who choose one of the ascetic ways of life, including that of celibacy, may be able to perceive from a distance meanings that are not apparent to those who view one or another aspect of life at close range. This possibility may be hard to imagine; it is analogous to the fact that in human speech the silences between words are required to distinguish one word from another, and thus to convey the meaning of sentences. Both words and silences are necessary if the expression is to make sense. The Christian insight may be that it takes both life styles—sexually active and celibate—to express the fullness of what it means to be human.

These nine points have represented only hints of how one might rethink the issues of personal and social behavior. My concern has been not to restructure the moral guidelines, but to rethink the foundations on which those guidelines rest. Perhaps enough has been said to suggest, as well, that any moral advice worthy of the Christian tradition is also a form of spiritual guidance. Sexuality and spirituality intersect in the person. For Christians, spirituality is not "immateriality" but *Spirit*uality, that is, the growth of the whole person toward the immanent and transcendent Being whose love is at the heart of the universe. That love is the same love one looks for in self-pleasuring, in the intimacy of friendship, and in the ultimate act of sexual ecstasy.

The view that sexual relationships should be publicly assessed according to criteria different from those applicable to other human relationships is now beginning to fade. With it will go the notion that sexual relationships limit one to a minimal spirituality and a preventive morality. The "Mardi Gras syndrome" will give way to an authentic and enriching Christian view of sexuality.

Notes

Introduction

1. For example, rape centers have not been able to get funding in Congress, for they are considered "women's issues." If such centers are ever funded, it will be because political maneuvering has been able to get consideration for them as part of a mental health program. See *Sexuality Today Newsletter* 4, no. 12 (12 January 1981): 1.

Chapter 2 / Friday: Sweeping the House

1. See, for example, Herant Katchadourian and Donald T. Lunde, *Fundamentals of Human Sexuality* (New York: Holt, Rinehart and Winston, 1980), or Bryan Strong et al., *Human Sexuality: Essentials,* 2nd edition (St. Paul: West Publishing Co., 1981). It is essential to have access to and to read thoroughly one of the comprehensive and responsible treatments of human sexuality from the points of view of the physical and social sciences.

2. There is a glaring inconsistency in the fact that the Middle Ages, following the Epistle of Barnabas, cautioned human beings *not* to be like the hare, hyena, or weasel. These animals were not to be eaten and were associated mostly with homosexuality because of what was believed to be their "unnatural sexual behavior." (It appears then that there was a standard within the standard, that is, some animals are more natural than others!) It was also largely ignored that animals such as cows and horses who copulate only when impregnation is pos-

sible are also incestuous and promiscuous. These inconsistencies were noticed, of course, and by the time of Thomas Aquinas in the thirteenth century, only certain species of birds, committed to lifelong monogamy, were used as models of "natural behavior." Woody Allen continues the "tradition," referring to the permanence of the mariage bond as the province of "pigeons and Catholics."

3. A modern example of this attitude is Freud's description of the difference between men and women as the "missing penis." This is, of course, no more reasonable than to assume that men are to be defined by the "missing uterus."

4. Richard A. McCormick, S.J., *How Brave a New World: Dilemmas in Bioethics* (Garden City, N.Y.: Doubleday and Co., 1981), p. 17.

5. For example, in Hennepin County, Minnesota, only ten out of three thousand acts of sexual abuse of children came to court in 1982. Convictions were delivered and the perpetrators were imprisoned. Most such acts are either unreported, remain unprosecuted, or the sentences given amount to no more than a visit to a psychiatrist. There are even cases on record where the local community protected the abuser and refused to admit the seriousness and criminal character of imposing adult sexual advances on children. And Hennepin County is one of the leaders in the nation in prosecuting child abuse.

6. Avery Dulles, "The Theologian and the Magisterium, "*Proceedings of the Catholic Theological Society of America* 31 (1976): 246.

Chapter 3 / Saturday: Hiding the Treasure

1. Irenaeus continued with a kind of definition of what it means to be truly alive: "true life, however, is the vision of God." His understanding of the "vision of God" needs to be interpreted as well. I believe I am using it here fairly, for the sacramental vision of God in this life is as real as the so-called "beatific" vision of God. Moreover, one could supplement the static imagery of "seeing" God with the dynamic imagery of "knowing" God, as Augustine says, not face to face, but "mouth to mouth."

2. At this point in history there is no evidence that Christians aspired to imitate Jesus in virginity. Celibacy emerges as a value much later. The logic is this: since physical martyrdom and death are not

available to all, celibacy as a kind of martyrdom is accepted in imitation of Jesus' martyrdom.

3. Note how very different is this motivation for abstinence from that of St. Paul, for whom sex is holy, but because the world is ending, there are more important things.

4. Had Jesus been born of a sexual act, according to Augustine, the sinful state of concupiscence would have been transmitted to him. The distance from Paul to Augustine is once again dramatic. Paul too believed that sin was handed on from one generation to the next through the "flesh," but for him "flesh" means choices contrary to the reign of God. He does not see the sexual act as evil or responsible for passing on original sin and its effects. Neither did he need a doctrine of the virgin birth. Christ was Lord, for Paul, because of his relation to God, not because of his alleged asexual origins.

5. The Eastern churches never developed the practice of daily eucharistic liturgy. It is instructive that their clergy marry to this day.

6. These were the reasons for which one entered a monastery. Since the monks were not priests, ritual purity by abstaining from women was not part of the motivation for their vows. It was response to a perceived gift of God which called them as individuals to a particular way of life.

7. John Boswell, *Social Tolerance, Homosexuality, and Christianity* (Chicago: University of Chicago Press, 1981), p. 163.

8. Peter Lombard, *PL* 192, 920 (*The Sentences* 3, 31,6).

9. St. Bernard, in his 65th Sermon on the Song of Songs writes: "To attack marriage is to open the doors to the debauchery of concubinaries, perpetrators of incest, *seminiflues, masculoru, concubitores* for chastity cannot be imposed on everyone." It was conventional for translators to leave provocative words such as "masturbators" and "Sodomites" untranslated.

10. The positive side of the Church's insistence that marriages should not be concluded with impediments, such as kinship, was expressed by Gratian in his *Decretum* (c. 35, q. 5, c. 2). Canonical impediments, he observed, encouraged families to contract marriages outside the kin group in order to widen the sway of that *caritas* which is natural within the family group.

11. Georges Duby, *Medieval Marriage: Two Models from Twelfth Century France* (Baltimore: Johns Hopkins University Press, 1978,

p. 19). The times when sexual intercourse was forbidden were many though they varied from place to place. Usually, it was forbidden during Lent, three days before receiving communion, and as noted earlier, from Thursday through Monday of each week. In the most rigorous dioceses, only forty days of the year remained free of prohibitions.

12. In the register of punishments inflicted in the rural deanery of Droitwich in 1300, 106 out of 107 persons who were condemned to public whipping were punished for adultery or fornication. Sin and sex practically coincided in the public mind.

13. There were even cases in which the unions were dissolved since it was agreed that in them "*dilectio* is impossible."

Chapter 4 / Sunday: Lighting the Lamp

1. Everett William, "Between Augustine and Hildebrand: A Critical Response to Human Sexuality," *Proceedings of the Catholic Theological Society of America* 33 (1978): 79.

2. Margaret Farley, "The Church and the Family: An Ethical Task," *Horizons* 10, no. 1 (1983): 59.

3. Lewis Thomas, *The Medusa and the Snail* (New York: Viking Press, 1979), pp. 82–87.

4. It would be illuminating to explore the ration between dehumanizing sexual expression and the level of unemployment in a society. Such anonymous and dehumanizing sex is used to avoid rather than seek intimacy.

Chapter 5 / Monday: Buying the Field

1. John Dunne, *Time and Myth* (Garden City, N.Y.: Doubleday and Co., 1973), p. 66.

Chapter 6 / Tuesday: Finding the Coin

1. Mary Douglas in *Purity and Danger* (Boston: Routledge & Kegan Paul, 1978) suggests that "when rituals express anxiety about

the body's orifices the sociological counterpart of this anxiety is a care to protect the political and cultural unity of a minority group. The Israelites were always a hard-pressed minority. In their beliefs all the bodily issues were polluting, blood, pus, excreta, semen, etc. The threatened boundaries of their body politic would be well mirrored in their care for the integrity, unity and purity of the physical body . . . . It is a symbolic system, based on the image of the body, whose primary concern is the ordering of a social hierarchy" (p. 124).

"The rituals enact the form of social relations and in giving these relations visible expression they enable people to know their own society. The rituals work upon the body politic through the symbolic medium of the physical body" (p. 128).

Chapter 7 / Wednesday: Calling the Neighbors

1. Marie Augusta Neal, "Sociology and Sexuality: A Feminist Perspective," *Christianity and Crisis* 39, no. 8 (1979): 121.

2. The "finality of the sexual act" or the "finality of the faculty" is supposedly the principal criterion of its morality, according to the Vatican's *Declaration on Certain Questions Concerning Sexual Ethics* (*Origins* 5, no. 31 [22 January 1976]: 488, 490). This finality, though not explicitly defined here is taken to be insemination, which itself is assumed to mean fertilization.

3. This was said in the context of action for the elimination of injustices, a context in which the critique of sexual mentality, customs, laws, and structures should also take place.

4. "Legal sources reflect the fact that the structure of the family has changed from a father-controlled system to one based on equality of the parents. Development of family law from 1850 to present, for instance, reflects the emergence of the married woman as a legal personality. In general, the disabilities imposed upon her under common law have been removed by legislation or judicial option. The child still occupies nearly the status he had under common law, although legal developments are contributing to the emergence of the child as a person in his own right. Exceptions to his inferior legal status are already found in the support laws. The child's legal right to support from both his parents is now recognized. Furthermore, the prevailing standard for

awarding custody to child-custody cases is in the best interests of the child." *Sex, Marriage, and Family: A Contemporary Christian Perspective*, ed. C.W. Tilberg (New York: Commission on Marriage, Board of Social Ministry, Lutheran Church of America, 1970), p. 20.

5. This is not to say that every individual human being must be active in a genital relationship. The absence or nonuse of a quality in individuals does not refute its normative character for the whole of humanity, as, for example, in such abnormalities as deafness, or the lack of reasonable intelligence, or in instances of nonuse such as of language or religion. Such exceptions do not affect the status of language, religion, or reason as constitutive elements of human life.

Recommended Readings

Chapter 1

Bailey, Derrick S. *The Man-Woman Relation in Christian Thought.* London: Longmans, Green and Co., 1959.

_____. *The Mystery of Love and Marriage: A Study in the Theology of Sexual Relations.* New York: Harper and Brothers, 1952.

Balthasar, Hans Urs von. *Love Alone.* New York: Herder and Herder, 1969.

Boff, Leonardo, O.F.M. "The Sacrament of Marriage." In *The Sacraments*, edited by Michael J. Taylor, S.J., pp. 193-204. New York: Alba House, 1981.

Bro, B. "Man and the Sacraments: The Anthropological Substructure of the Christian Sacraments." In *The Sacraments in General: A New Perspective. Concilium* 31, pp. 18-26. New York: Paulist Press, 1968.

Cooke, Bernard. *Sacraments and Sacramentality.* Mystic, Conn.: Twenty-third Publications, 1983.

Dupré, Louis. *The Other Dimension: A Search for the Meaning of Religious Attitude.* Garden City, N.Y.: Doubleday and Co., 1972.

Eliade, Mircea. *Cosmos and History: The Myth of the Eternal Return.* Translated by Willard Trask. New York: Harper, 1959.

_____. *A History of Religious Ideas.* Vol. 1, *From the Stone Age to the Eleusinian Mysteries*, translated by Willard R. Trask. Chicago: University of Chicago Press, 1978.

_____. *Images and Symbols: Studies in Religious Symbolism.* New York: Sheed and Ward, 1969.

_____. *The Sacred and the Profane.* Translated by Willard Trask. New York: Harper and Row, 1961.

Foucault, Michel. *The History of Sexuality.* Vol. 1. New York: Pantheon Books, 1978.

Greeley, Andrew. *Religion in the Year 2000.* New York: Sheed and Ward, 1969.

Haughton, Rosemary. *Tales From Eternity: The World of Fairy Tales and the Spiritual Search.* New York: Seabury Press, 1973.

Kilmartin, Edward J., S.J. "When Is Marriage a Sacrament?" *Theological Studies* 34 (1973): 275-86.

Lawler, Michael G. "Christian Rituals: An Essay in Sacramental Symbolism." *Horizons* 7, no. 1 (1980): 7-35.

Long, Charles H. *Alpha: The Myths of Creation.* New York: George Braziller, 1963.

Nelson, James B. *Embodiment: An Approach to Sexuality and Christian Theology.* Minneapolis: Augsburg Publishing House, 1978.

Perera, Sylvia Brinton. *Descent to the Goddess.* Toronto: Inner City Books, 1981.

Shea, John. "Human Experience and Religious Symbolization." *Ecumenist* 9, no. 4 (1971): 49-52.

Simons, G. L. *Sex and Superstition.* New York. Barnes and Noble Books, 1973.

Stone, Merlin. *When God Was a Woman.* New York: Dial Press, 1976.

Tannahil, Reay. *Sex in History.* Briarcliff Manor, N.Y.: Stein and Day, 1980.

Chapter 2

Berrill, N.J. *Sex and the Nature of Things.* New York: Dodd, Mead and Co., 1953.

Boston Women's Health Collective. *Our Bodies, Ourselves.* New York: Simon and Schuster, 1976.

Brecher, Edward. *The Sex Researchers.* Boston: Little, Brown and Co., 1969.

Bryant, M. Darrol. "Revolution and World Pluralism." *Ecumenist* 10, no. 3 (1972): 38-41.

Greeley, Andrew. *The Young Catholic Family*. Chicago: Thomas More Press, 1980.

Hite, Shere. *The Hite Report*. New York: Dell Publishing Co., 1977.

Katchadourian, Herant, and Lunde, Donald T. *Fundamentals of Human Sexuality*. New York: Holt, Rinehart and Winston, 1980.

Lasch, Christopher. *Haven in a Heartless World: The Family Besieged*. New York: Basic Books, 1977.

Masters, William H.; Johnson, Virginia; and Kolodny, Robert. *Human Sexuality*. Boston: Little, Brown and Co., 1982.

McCary, James Leslie. *Human Sexuality*. 2nd brief ed. New York: D. Van Nostrand Co. 1979.

Mead, Margaret. *Male and Female*. New York: Dell Publishing Co., 1968.

Montagu, Ashley. *Touching: The Human Significance of the Skin*. New York: Harper and Row, 1972.

Offit, Avodah. *Night Thoughts: Reflections of a Sex Therapist*. Congdon and Lattes, 1981.

"The Redbook Report: A Study of Female Sexuality." *Redbook* 145 (October 1975): 38ff.

Romano, Deborah Larned. "Sexual Confidence." *McCall's* 107, no. 12 (September 1980): 113.

Sorenson, Robert C. *Adolescent Sexuality in Contemporary America: The Sorenson Report: Personal Values and Sexual Behavior Ages 13-19*. New York: World Publishing Co., 1973.

Strong, Bryan, et al. *Human Sexuality: Essentials*. 2nd edition. St. Paul, Minn.: West Publishing Co., 1981.

Westoff, Leslie Aldridge, and Westoff, Charles F. *From Now to Zero: Fertility, Contraception and Abortion in America*. Boston: Little, Brown and Co., 1968.

Wilson, Sam, et al. *Human Sexuality*. St. Paul, Minn.: West Publishing Co., 1980.

Chapter 3

Allen, William F. *Sexuality Summary*. Confield, Ohio: Alba Books, 1977.

Arntz, Joseph T., O.P. "Natural Law and Its History." In *Moral Prob-

lems and Christian Personalism. Concilium 5, pp. 39–57. New York: Paulist Press, 1965.

Ashe, Geoffrey. *The Virgin*. Boston: Routledge and Kegan Paul, 1976.

Augustine, *Confessions*. Garden City, N.Y.: Doubleday and Co., 1960.

_____. *Commentary on the Lord's Sermon on the Mount*, bk. I ch. 15. In *The Fathers of the Church*, vol. 11, translated Denis J, Kavanaugh, pp. 61–62. New York: Fathers of the Church, 1951.

Blenkinsopp, Joseph. *Sexuality and the Christian Tradition*. Dayton: Pflaum Press, 1969.

Boswell, John. *Christianity, Social Tolerance, and Homosexuality: Gay People in Western Europe from the Beginning of the Christian Era to the Fourteenth Century*. Chicago: University of Chicago Press, 1980.

Brundage, James. "Prostitution in Medieval Canon Law." *Signs: Journal of Women* 1, no. 4 (1976): 825–45.

Cairncross, John. *After Polygamy Was Made a Sin: The Social History of Christian Polygamy*. Boston: Routledge and Kegan Paul, 1974.

Cole, William Graham. *Sex in Christianity and Psychoanalysis*. New York: Oxford University Press, 1966.

Curran, Charles. "Sexuality and Sin: A Current Appraisal." In *Contemporary Problems in Moral Theology*. Notre Dame, Ind.: Fides Publications, 1970.

Dodds, E. R. *Pagan and Christian in an Age of Anxiety*. New York: W. W. Norton and Co., 1970.

Doherty, Dennis, ed. *Dimensions of Human Sexuality*. Garden City, N.Y.: Doubleday and Co., 1979.

Douglas, Mary. *Purity and Danger*. Boston: Routledge and Kegan Paul, 1978.

_____. ed. *Rules and Meanings: The Anthropology of Everyday Knowledge*, Harmondsworth, England: Penguin Education, 1973.

Duby, Georges. *Medieval Marriage: Two Models from Twelfth Century France*. Translated by Elborg Forster. Baltimore: Johns Hopkins University Press, 1978.

Everett, William. "Between Augustine and Hildebrand: A Critical Response to Human Sexuality." *Proceedings of the Catholic Theological Society of America* 33 (1978): 77–83.

Ferrante, Joan. *Woman as Image in Medieval Literature from the Twelfth Century to Dante*. New York: Columbia University Press, 1975.

Fuchs, Joseph. *Die Sexualethik des heiligen Thomas von Aquin*. Köln: Bachem, 1949.

Grant, Robert M. *Augustine to Constantine: The Thrust of the Christian Movement into the Roman World*. New York: Harper and Row, 1970.

Greeley, Andrew. "Church Authority: Beyond the Problem." *National Catholic Reporter*, September 26, 1980, pp. 7-9.

Heidel, Alexander. *The Babylonian Genesis*. Chicago: University of Chicago Press, 1951.

Human Life Center, *A Reader in Natural Family Planning*, No. 1. 2d ed. Collegeville: St. John's University, 1978.

Human Sexuality and Personhood. Proceedings of the Worksop for the Hierarchies of the United States and Canada sponsored by the Pope John XXIII Medical-Moral Research and Education Center, Dallas, Texas, February 2-6, 1981. St. Louis, Mo.: Pope John XXIII Center, 1981.

Jerome, "Ep. X, ad Lucinum." In *Lettres*, edited and translated by Jerome Labourt. 8 vols. Paris: Les Belles Lettres, 1949-1963. 4:71.

――――. "Epistle lxxvii." In *Select Letters of St. Jerome*, edited by F. A. Wright. The Loeb Classical Library. London: W. Heinemann, 1954.

Kerns, Joseph. *Theology of Marriage*. New York: Sheed and Ward, 1964.

Laeuchli, Samuel. *Power and Sexuality*. Philadelphia: Temple University Press, 1972.

Macquarrie, John. "Rethinking Natural Law." In *Readings in Moral Theology No. 2*, edited by Charles Curran and Richard McCormick, S.J. New York: Paulist Press, 1980.

Matthews, Robert J. *The Human Adventure: A Study Course for Christians on Sexuality*. Lima, Ohio: C.S.S. Publishing Co., 1980.

McLaughlin, Eleanor, "The Christian Past: Does It Hold a Future for Women?" In *Womanspirit Rising*, pp. 93-106. New York: Harper Forum Book, 1979.

Murphy, Francis X. "Of Sex and the Catholic Church." *Atlantic Monthly* 247 (February 1981): 44-45.

Murstein, Bernard I. *Love, Sex, and Marriage Through the Ages.* New York: Springer Publishing Co., 1974.

Noonan, John T. *Contraception: A History of Its Treatment by the Catholic Theologians and Canonists.* Cambridge: Harvard University Press, 1966.

_____. ed. *The Morality of Abortion.* Cambridge: Harvard University Press, 1970.

Parrinder, Geoffrey. *Sex in the World's Religions.* New York: Oxford University Press, 1980.

Riga, Peter J. *Sexuality and Marriage in Recent Catholic Thought.* Washington, D.C.: Corpus Papers, 1969.

Ruether, Rosemary Radford, ed. *Religion and Sexism: Images of Women in the Jewish and Christian Tradition.* New York: Simon and Schuster, 1979.

_____, and McLaughlin, Eleanor. *Women of Spirit: Female Leadership in the Jewish and Christian Tradition.* New York: Simon and Schuster, 1979.

Runciman, Steven. *The Medieval Manichee: A Study of the Christian Dualist Heresy.* Cambridge: Cambridge University Press, 1960.

Schillebeeckx, Edward. *Ministry.* New York: Crossroad Publishing Co., 1981.

Sieverth, Gustav. "The Doctrine of Original Sin Developed and Presented in Accordance with the Theology of St. Thomas Aquinas." In *Sin,* edited by Marc Oraison et al., pp. 128–48. New York: Macmillan Publishing Co., 1962.

Taylor, Michael, ed. *Sex: Thoughts for Contemporary Christians.* Garden City, N.Y.: Doubleday and Co., 1972.

Tertullian, "The Apparel of Women." In *Disciplinary, Moral, and Ascetical Works,* bk. 1. New York: The Fathers of the Church, 1959.

_____. "To His Wife." In *Treatises on Marriage and Remarriage.* Ancient Christian Writers, vol. 13, pp. 35ff. Westminster, Md.: Newman Press, 1956.

von Hildebrand, Dietrich. "Marriage and Overpopulation." *Thought* 36 (1961): 81–100.

Chapter 4

Baum, Gregory. "Catholic Homosexuals." *Commonweal* 99 (1974). 479–82.

———. *The Social Imperative.* New York: Paulist Press, 1979.

Becken, Alfons. *Process and Permanence in Ethics: Max Scheler's Moral Philosophy.* New York: Paulist Press, 1974.

Buckley, Mary. "The Rising of Woman Is the Rising of the Race." *Proceeding of the Catholic Theological Society of America* 34 (1979): 48–63.

Cahill, Lisa. "Sexual Issues in Christian Theological Ethics: A Review of Recent Studies." *Religious Studies Review* 4, no. 1 (1978).

"Child Abuse: Society's Symptom of Stress." *Christianity Today* 21 (1977): 6–8.

Christ, Carol, and Plaskow, Judith, eds. *Womanspirit Rising.* New York: Harper and Row, 1979.

Daly, Mary. *Beyond God the Father.* Boston: Beacon Press, 1973.

Farley, Margaret A., "New Patterns of Relationship: Beginnings of a Moral Revolution." *Theological Studies* 36 (1975): 627–46.

Freire, Paulo. *The Pedagogy of the Oppressed.* New York: Herder and Herder, 1970.

Gilligan, Carol. "In a Different Voice: Women's Conceptions of Self and of Morality." *Harvard Educational Review* 47, no. 4 (1977): 481–516.

———. "Woman's Place in Man's Life Cycle." *Harvard Educational Review* 49, no. 4 (1979): 431–46.

Goldenberg, Judith Plaskow. *The Coming of Lilith: Toward a Feminist Theology.* Loveland: Ohio: Grailville, 1972.

Grace, James H., ed. *God, Sex and the Social Project.* The Glassboro Papers on Religion and Sexuality. New York: Edwin Mellen Press, 1978.

Hageman, Alice L., ed. *Sexist Religion and Women in the Church: No More Silence!* New York: Association Press, 1974.

Holland, Joe, and Henriot, Peter, S.J. *Social Analysis: Linking Faith and Justice.* Washington, D.C.: Center of Concern, 1980.

Keane, Philip S. *Sexual Morality: A Catholic Perspective.* New York: Paulist Press, 1977.

Kelly, William J., ed. *Theology and Discovery: Essays in Honor of Karl Rahner, S.J.* Milwaukee: Marquette University Press, 1980.

Kennedy, Eugene. *The New Sexuality: Myths, Fables and Hangups.* Garden City, N.Y.: Doubleday and Co., 1972.

_____. *What a Modern Catholic Believes About Sex.* Chicago: Thomas More Press, 1971.

Kirkendall, Lester. *A New Bill of Sexual Rights and Responsibilities.* New York: Prometheus Books, 1977.

Kosnik, Anthony, et al. *Human Sexuality: New Directions in American Catholic Thought.* A study commissioned by the Catholic Theological Society of America. New York: Paulist Press, 1977.

MacKinnon, Catherine A. "Feminism, Marxism and the State: Toward Feminist Jurisprudence." *Signs* 8, no. 4 (1983): 635-58.

Maguire, Daniel C. "Human Sexuality: The Book and the Epiphenomenon," *Proceedings of the Catholic Theological Society of America* 33 (1978): 54-76.

_____. *The Moral Choice.* New York: Doubleday and Co., 1978.

McGrath, Sr. Albertus Magnus, O.P. *What a Modern Catholic Believes About Women.* Chicago: Thomas More Press, 1972.

Murphy, Francis X., and Earhart, Joseph. "Catholic Perspectives on Population Issues." *The Population Bulletin* 30, no. 6. Washington, D.C.: Population Reference Bureau, 1975.

Naisbitt, John. "The New Economic and Political Order of the 1980's." *Aide* 11, no. 3 (Fall 1980): 10-15.

Neal, Sr. Marie Augusta. "A Turning Point of Religious Ethics." *Ecumenist* 16 (1977): 5-8.

Omoregbe, Joseph. "Evolution in Bernard Haring's Ethical Thinking." *Louvain Studies* 7, no. 1 (1978): 45-54.

Petras, John. *Sexuality in Society.* Boston: Allyn and Bacon, 1973.

Pierce, Christine. "Natural Law, Language and Women." *Women in Sexist Society*, edited by Vivian Gornick and Barbara K. Moran, pp. 242-58. New York: Signet Books, 1972.

Rahner, Karl. "Pluralism in Theology and the Oneness of the Church's Profession of Faith." In *The Development of Fundamental Theology. Concilium* 46, pp. 103-23. New York: Paulist Press, 1969.

Roszak, Betty and Roszak, Theodore. *Masculine/Feminine: Readings in Sexual Mythology and the Liberation of Women.* New York: Harper and Row, 1969.

Ruether, Rosemary Radford. "The Call of Women in the Church Today." *Listening: Journal of Religion and Culture* 15, no. 3 (1980): 241-49.

———. *Mary: The Feminine Face of the Church*. Philadelphia: Westminster Press, 1977.

Selling, Joseph A. "Moral Teaching, Traditional Teaching and Humanae Vitae." *Louvain Studies* 17, no. 1 (1978): 24-44.

Steinfels, Peter. "Sex and Liberation." *Commonweal* 103 (1976): 560ff.

Thompson, Thomas L. "Book Review of Anthony Kosnik et al., Human Sexuality: New Directions in American Catholic Thought." *Journal of Ecumenical Studies* 16, no. 4 (1979): 773-75.

Tilberg, Cedric W., ed. *Sex, Marriage and Family: A Contemporary Christian Perspective*. New York: Commission on Marriage, Board of Social Ministry, Lutheran Church of America, 1970.

Tracy, David. "On Galatians 3:28." *Criterion* 16, no. 3 (1977): 10-12.

Ulanov, Ann Bedford. *The Feminine in Jungian Psychology and in Christian Theology*. Evanston, Ill.: Northwestern University Press, 1971.

Valente, Michael F. *Sex: The Radical View of a Catholic Theologian*. Milwaukee: Bruce Publishing Co., 1970.

Zaretsky, E. *Capitalism, the Family and Personal Life*. New York: Harper and Row, 1976.

Chapter 5

Baker, Robert, and Elliston, Frederick, eds. *Philosophy and Sex*. Buffalo: Prometheus Books, 1977.

Davis, Charles. *Body as Spirit: The Nature of Religious Feeling*. New York: Seabury Press, 1976.

Dennerstein, Lorraine, et al. *Gynecology, Sex, and Psyche*. Melbourne, Australia: Melbourne University Press, 1978.

Dunne, John. *Time and Myth*. Garden City, N.Y.: Doubleday and Co., 1973.

Gittleson, Natalie. "Sexual Delight: How to Keep It Alive in Your Marriage." *McCall's* 107, no. 11 (August 1980): 204.

Greeley, Andrew. *Love and Play*. New York: Seabury Press, 1977.

Hart, Thomas N. *Living Happily Ever After: Toward a Theology of Christian Marriage.* New York: Paulist Press, 1979.

Julian of Norwich. *Revelations of Divine Love.* Translated and edited by Clifton Walters. Baltimore: Penguin Books, 1966.

Keen, Sam. "Manifesto for a Dionysian Theology." In *Transcendence*, edited by Herbert Richardson and Donald Cutler, pp. 51ff. Boston: Beacon Press, 1969.

Kelling, George W. *Blind Mazes: A Study of Love.* Chicago: Nelson-Hall 1980.

Lawler, Justus George. *Celestial Pantomime: Poetic Structures of Transcendence*, pp. 207-63. New Haven: Yale University Press, 1979.

O'Brien, David J., and Shannon, Thomas A., eds. *Renewing the Earth.* New York: Doubleday Image Books, 1977.

Outka, Gene. *Agape: An Ethical Analysis.* New Haven: Yale University Press, 1972.

Rosenstock-Huessy, Eugen. *Out of Revolution: Autobiography of a Western Man.* Norwich, Vt.: Argo Books, 1969.

Thomas, Lewis. *The Medusa and the Snail.* New York: Viking Press, 1979.

Watts, Alan W. *Nature, Man and Woman.* New York: Pantheon Books, 1958.

Williams, Daniel Day. *The Spirit and the Forms of Love.* New York: Harper and Row, 1968.

Chapter 6

Barth, Karl. *Church Dogmatics.* Vol. III/1, pp. 191-206. Edinburgh: T. & T. Clark, 1961.

Barr, James. "The Meaning of 'Mythology' in Relation to the Old Testament." *Vetus Testamentum* 9 (1959): 1-10.

Bird, Joseph W., and Bird, Lois F. *The Freedom of Sexual Love: A Christian Concept of Sexuality in Marriage.* New York: Doubleday and Co., 1967.

Brown, Raymond. "The Problem of the Virginal Conception of Jesus." *Theological Studies* 33 (1972): 3-25.

Driver, Tom. "Sexuality and Jesus." In *New Theology No. 3*, edited by Martin E. Marty and Dean Peerman. New York: Macmillan Publishing Co., 1966.

Goergen, Donald, O.P. *The Sexual Celibate*. New York: Seabury Press, 1975.

Gollwitzer, Helmut. *Song of Love: A Biblical Understanding of Sex*. Philadelphia: Fortress Press, 1979.

Gordis, Robert. *Love and Sex: The Jewish Perspective*. New York: Farrar, Straus and Giroux, 1978.

Kelsey, David H. *The Uses of Scripture in Recent Theology*. Philadelphia: Fortress Press, 1975.

Landy, Francis. "The Song of Songs and the Garden of Eden." *Journal of Biblical Literature* 98, no. 4 (1979): 513-28.

McNeill, John J., S.J. *The Church and the Homosexual*. Kansas City: Sheed, Andrews and McMeel, 1976.

Phipps, William E. "The Plight of the Song of Songs." *Journal of the American Academy of Religion* 42, no. 1 (1974): 82-101.

_____. *The Sexuality of Jesus*. New York: Harper and Row, 1973.

Chapter 7

Barnhouse, Ruth Tiffany, and Holmes, Urban T., III, eds. *Male and Female: Christian Approaches to Sexuality*. New York: Seabury Press, 1976.

Baum, Gregory. "Catholic Homosexuals." *Commonweal* 99 (1974): 479-82.

Böckle, Franz. "Birth Control: A Survey of German, French, and Dutch Literature on Birth Control." In *Moral Problems and Christian Personalism. Concilium* 5, pp. 97-129. New York: Paulist Press, 1965.

_____, and Pohier, Jacques-Marie, eds. *Sexuality in Contemporary Catholicism. Concilium* 100. New York: Seabury Press, 1976.

Curran, Charles E. and McCormick, Richard A., S.J., eds. *Readings in Moral Theology No. 2: The Distinctiveness of Christian Ethics*. New York: Paulist Press, 1950.

Darst, David, and Forgue, Joseph. "Sexuality on the Island Earth." *Ecumenist* 7, no. 6 (1969): 81-87.

Diamond, James, J., M.D. "Abortion, Animation, and Biological Hominization. *Theological Studies* 36 (1975): 305-24.

Dominian, Jack. *The Church and the Sexual Revolution*. Denville, N.J.: Dimension Books, 1971.

Farley, Margaret A. "The Church and the Family: An Ethical Task." *Horizons* 10, no. 1 (1983): 50-71.

Forster, Robert, and Orest, Ranum, eds. *Family and Society*. Baltimore: Johns Hopkins University Press, 1976.

Garvey, John, and Morriss, Frank. *Catholic Perspectives: Abortion*. Chicago: Thomas More Press, 1979.

Häring, Bernard. *Ethics of Manipulation*. New York: Seabury Press, 1975.

_____. *Free and Faithful in Christ: Moral Theology for Clergy and Laity*. 3 vols. New York: Crossroad Publishing Co., 1978-1981.

_____. *The Law of Christ*. 3 vols. Westminster, Md.: Newman Press, 1964.

_____. *Morality Is for Persons*. New York: Farrar, Straus and Giroux, 1971.

_____. *Shalom: Peace*. New York: Doubleday Image Books, 1969.

Katz, Joseph, and Cronin, Denise M. "Sexualilty and College Life." *Change* 12, no. 2 (1980): 44-49.

Mackey, James. *Modern Theology of Tradition*. New York: Herder and Herder, 1962.

McCormick, Richard A., S.J. *How Brave a New World: Dilemmas in Bioethics*. Garden City, N.Y. Doubleday and Co., 1981.

Milhaven, J. G. "The Voice of Lay Experience in Christian Ethics." *Proceedings of the Catholic Theological Society of America* 33 (1978): 35-53.

Neal, Sr. Marie Augusta. "Sociology and Sexuality: A Feminist Perspective." *Christiantity and Crisis* 39, no. 8 (1979): 118-25.

Nugent, Robert, ed. *A Challenge to Love: Gay and Lesbian Catholics in the Church*. New York: Crossroad Publishing Co., 1983.

Pittenger, Norman. *A Time for Consent: A Christian's Approach to Homosexuality*. New York: Oxford University Press, 1976.

Rahner, Karl. "The Church's Limits." In *The Christian of the Future*, pp. 49-76. New York: Herder and Herder, 1967.

Small, Dwight Hervey. *Christian: Celebrate Your Sexuality*. Old Tappan, N.J.: Fleming H. Revell, 1974.

Srnedes, Lewis B. *Sex for Christians: The Limits and Liberties of Sexual Living*. Grand Rapids: Wm. B. Edermans Publishing Co., 1976.

Tracy, David. "Theology as Public Discourse." *The Christian Century* 92, no. 10 (1975): 280-84.

The United Church of Christ. *Human Sexuality: A Preliminary Study*. New York: United Church Press, 1977.

Wagner, Richard, O.M.I. "Being Gay and Celibate — Another View." *National Catholic Reporter* 12, no. 5 (November 21, 1980): 16.

Williams, Daniel Day. "Three Studies of Homosexuality in Relation to the Christian Faith." *Social Action* 34 (1967): 30-39.

Woods, Richard, O.P. *Another Kind of Love: Homosexuality and Spirituality*. Chicago: Thomas More Association, 1977.